Dedicated to:

The MATULigans - those graduates from the MATUL who have continued in their quest to establish the Kingdom in the darkest places globally.

Other books by Viv Grigg:

The Lifestyle and Values of Servants
Companion to the Poor
Cry of the Urban Poor
Towards an Auckland Business Theology (Ed)
The Spirit of Christ and the Postmodern City
Kiwinomics: Conversations with New Zealand's Economic Soul

ISBN:.978-0-9582019-8-8

Published by: Urban Leadership Foundation
P. O. Box 68-244
Wellesley Street
Auckland 1141
 New Zealand

admin@urbanleaders.org
www.urbanleaders.org/ma
www.matul.org

Revised Edition

SLUM DWELLERS' THEOLOGY

PEDAGOGY IN THE SLUMS

Viv Grigg

urban leadership foundation

Part 1: HISTORY

Introduction
Innovations in Theological Education

EXPLORING INNOVATIVE EDUCATIONAL FRAMEWORKS

01

FOLLOWING THE URBAN SPIRIT

02

PATHWAY TO THE SEMINARY IN THE SLUMS

Page 12

The Call

Is There a Problem?

Subsidiary questions

Research Methodology

The Flow of Argument

Acknowledgements

Page 19

The 1980's: The Voice Calling, Birthing

History's Echoing Voice

The 1990's: Indigenous Urban Poor Missions

The 2000's: Postmodern Learning Networks:.

The Millennial Future: Empowerment of Cross and Resurrection

The Spirit, Humility and Greater Works

Page 26

Genesis of the MATUL

Implementation of Process

Institutional Frustrations

Creative Expansion

Part 2: ANDRAGOGY

05

TRANSFORMATIONAL CONVERSATIONS - ANDRAGOGY WITH THE URBAN POOR

04

POOROLOGY: A DISCUSSION ON ANDRAGOGY WITH FREIRE AND JESUS

03

JESUS' SEMINARY IN THE SLUMS

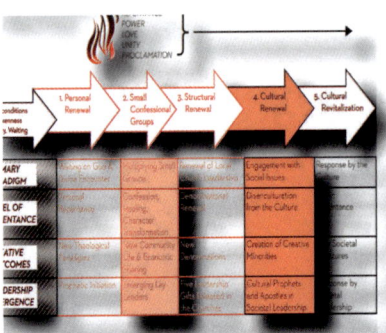

09

INTEGRATING THE NEW FIELD OF URBAN POOR SPIRITUALITY

𝒫art 4: INNOVATIVE EDUCATION

10

VOCATIONAL TRAINING MODELS

11

GRASSROOTS LEARNING NETWORKS

12

INNOVATIVE TECHNOLOGY IN URBAN MISSIOLOGICAL EDUCATION

13

VERTICALLY INTEGRATED DELIVERY SYSTEMS FOR URBAN POOR MISSIOLOGY

14

PLATFORMS FOR SCALING URBAN POOR MISSIOLOGICAL EDUCATION

15

PROPOSAL: EXPAND THE URBAN POOR LEADERS' TRAINING COMMISSION

16

FROM SLUM LEADERSHIP TO TRANSFORMATION OF POST-POSTMODERN MEGALOPOLISES

FINALE

Frontispiece

Viv Grigg, with HBI faculty and students

This is a book of dreams! This is a book of 100 dreams fulfilled, 1000 failed and the lessons learned! This is a book of 10,000 dreams yet to be fulfilled!

Theological education of urban poor leaders is at the foundation of cultural and values change. It is a little recognized time bomb in the liberation of the dispossessed into the productivity of societal transformation.

Movements in the slums are based on simple slogans by oral-culture leaders. How can we dream of getting the seminary into the slums, so that these leaders develop tools and skills, vision, values and global reference points to bring about liberty from oppression?

Walk with me and other brothers and sisters in these pages to explore our common dreams and the lessons learned in the pains of childbirth of an educational movement across continents.

This book is penned to assist presidents, deans and program directors as they seek to master how to structure this program. It is designed to help MATUL students grasp the dynamics of the program, and MATULigan graduates in finding their way to multiply training among the urban poor.

August 2018

New Paradigms & Innovations

Innovations in Theological Education

Getting the seminary in the slums

Transformational conversations as a theological methodology

Pedagogical Innovations for Creating Slum Leadership Training

Theology & vocational training models

Grassroots learning networks

Innovations in technological delivery systems

New Domain of Urban Poor Missiology

NEW FIELDS

Urban poor movement leadership

Urban poor social entrepreneurship

Urban poor spirituality

Innovations in Academic Communications

This book looks like a magazine, but don't be fooled!

It develops a number of new academic paradigms

Academics should be communicated graphically in a visual society!

Introduction:
Exploring
Innovative
Educational
Frameworks

One writes out of one thing only—one's own experience. Everything depends on how relentlessly one forces from this experience the last drop, sweet or bitter, it can possibly give. This is the only real concern of the artist, to recreate out of the disorder of life that order which is art.

-James Baldwin

The Call

Ateneo Park in Manila in 1976. I was 25. My first church-planting team were spending the day together seeking the Lord as to how we should plant the church in Kamuning. As I looked up at the only cloud in the sky I heard what was like a voice, "Unless you create a master's degree for slum leaders where they have space to think, they will not survive". That was it. Nothing fancy. No design. No structure. Just a command. I saw in that flash of time, that transformative movements among the poor would not eventuate without the training of movement leaders at a Master's-degree level.

It would take us 30 years to work out how to do it! First we had to live it! To pay the same price that workers in the slums pay. To struggle with all the issues from how to enter, to how to preach, to how to form churches. Leadership was yet a bigger challenge. And how to engage in the complexity of socio-economic and political issues.

Then years of recruiting workers, relocating them, training them and learning from them as we formed global and indigenous missions. All the time, thinking, writing, studying.

It wasn't until thirty years later that the *Encarnação Training Commission*, in a shared wonderful sense of unity around this vision of master's-level training launched the *MA in Transformational Urban Leadership* initially in three schools.

What's the Problem?

Yesterday, I received a text. *"Can I take your training? I am a trainer of church-planters in my Indian city.".*

"What is your degree," I asked. It was a good Indian degree but would not get him into a global university. I referred him to some Indian Seminaries deliver-

Peter Nischke, Viv Grigg, Corrie de Boer, Olivia Nassaka, Dean of Uganda Christian University Theology School, at the MATUL Commission in Manila

ing the MA in Transformational Urban Leadership.

"I cannot leave my place of ministry," he replied. I referred him to some of my material online, to read and determine what he would like to study.

"You mean I have to read it and determine what to study? Can you just tell me what to do?".

That frames the question of this study:

- The educated man or woman leader in the slum
- Unskilled in theology or leadership development
- Training others in church-planting
- In a context of economic dispossessions, social dislocation, political oppression, spiritual depravity.
- Needing simple training
- In their place of productivity

How do such trainers:.
- become trained? so they can train other leaders?
- to train elders and deacons/esses in the Kingdom of God that transforms spirits and bodies and environments? And see transformation of dispossession to prosperity, dislocation to community, oppression to liberation, depravity to integrity and celebration?

There are assumptions:
- Thousands of urban poor church movements among the 1.4 billion in the slums and 2 billion urban poor.
- The divine revelation of the Kingdom of God is THE good news that transforms every nook and cranny of society: its spirituality, its economics, its politics, its social structures, its geography (for slums are a geographic construct).
- Religious movements of congregating believers among the urban poor, who carry the Holy Spirit and preach this Kingdom are the cradle of hope, love and faith that enables transformation.
- There is no assumption that these local cradles are the ultimate sociology through which the values of the Kingdom move. Derivative civic organizations, social movements, business structures and governmental roles all can be transformative vehicles of the Kingdom and the Church.
- The context of the lower circuit sector, the slums, reflects the sins of the upper circuit, the globalized economy. So, in parallel, we have to explore the upper level education for the elites to engage oppression that creates the urban poverty.

The problem has a context. We have been talking of 1.4 billion in the slums for some years. Governments do not wish to indicate that figure has increased, but likely it has dramatically increased. Conservatively, we can talk of 2 billion poor.

This book thus paints on a grand canvas. Speed is of essence in missions! "That none should perish," drives us. Thus we keep exploring the mass multiplication of training, and the rapidity of multiplication through educational movements.

But while the context is the lower circuit economic sector, the slums are a simple reflection of the sins of the upper circuit, the globalized economy. So in parallel we have to explore the upper level development of education for the elites to engage the urban poor. This we touch on, but do not develop fully in the final chapter.

Thus the question of this book is:

What andragogy will most rapidly facilitate training leaders to multiply holistic church-planting movements that facilitate transforming the slums?

Subsidiary Questions.

The question implies others:

- **Content:** What is core content for grassroots mass multiplication and what is core content for upper level engagement with urban leadership?
- **Technology**: How can global technological structure foster local delivery?
- **Resourcing:** What level of diversified resourcing is needed for development and design of product?
- **Product:** What new products are needed and how do we leverage existing products?.
- **Language Barriers:** Of the mega-trade language groupings, how do we cross critical boundaries of language?
- **Opposition:** How do we overcome entrenched doctrinal enclaves of prosperity teaching and magic-based Christianity based on liturgy or rituals (be it Pentecostal or Anglican or Catholic)?
- **Movement Pathways:** What are the critical pathways to movements? multiplying church movements, multiplying social movements? What are the critical pathways to liberation or transformation? Multiple level training pathways are needed.
- **Collaboration:** To accomplish a wide goal, collaboration at multiple levels is needed.
- **Bottlenecks:** In the flow of processes, what are the bottlenecks? How do these define strategy?

- ***Educational Pathways***: How do we create educational pathways that enable the learners to pose their questions, but enables a ladder to more fundamental questions and broader theology and praxis.
- ***Accreditation Pathways***. The biggest barrier is always the issue of credibility. That is defined both nationally and internationally.

Research Methodology

We didn't set out to do research. But in reality this documents twenty years of action-reflection research. The study itself unintentionally uses the *Transformational Conversations Model* (explained in Chapter 5). This includes multiple cycles. Each cycle beginning with a cluster of activists implementing an idea, moving through evaluation and reflection to generate the next set of actions.

It is action research, as it begins with seeking to solve a problem. In the process new theory is developed. It is community-based action research, as we are engaging a community - the global urban poor - and recommending solutions to a community - the *Encarnação Alliance Training Commission.*

Each cycle begins with an action story, and ends with action outcomes.

The action story defines the theme of that particular cycle. The action outcomes lead to a new problem and cycle of action-reflection.

Each cycle involves a social sciences conversation of social or educational or contextual analysis, a Biblical conversation which leads to theological conversation, and these integrate to a new theological perspective which becomes a new series of collective actions outworking the new missiology. Thus we are doing theology in action.

This is the first in a three book series. This first book has to do with the educational philosophy behind the delivery of the MATUL and explores the expansion of a global vertically integrated educational framework. It include a personal perspective. It is designed in a coffee book style to be left around the MATUL office or training centre coffee table in an internet cafe in the slums, so that Slum Learning Network trainers, University presidents, boards, deans, directors, faculty, adjuncts and students can all be familiar with core concepts.

It is a collective pilgrimage but developed from a personal perspective as I seek to pass on the DNA of what we are doing. Parts of it I am pulling from pervious publications of mine into an integrated whole.

The second book will contain the core documents and forms of the *Encarnação Alliance Training Commission,* a handbook for program administrators and faculty. The third reflects course by course on delivery issues in each course and is a collective production from faculty globally.

Conversations in this Book

This book itself shows the nature of action-reflection research built around Transformational Conversations.

Entrance and Incarnation
In Chapter 1, I reflect on 40 years of personal engagement in the slums, each decade being a different conversation; the first ten in modelling and writing the paradigm of incarnational mission in the slums when evangelicals had no theology for this; the second, in multiplying holistic missions; the third in multiplying grassroots training, and creating the *Encarnação Alliance of Urban Poor Missions*; the fourth in multiplying graduate-level training in eight schools.

In Chapter 2, I explore the history of the MATUL Commission, as it has sought to establish a Masters for urban poor leadership globally.

Theological Conversations
In Chapter 3, I derive from Jesus' educational style, the content of the 15 courses in the MATUL degree. In Chapter 4, I extend the Pedagogy of Jesus, into a discussion with Friere and Jesus on *andragogy* (adult education) among the dispossessed. Chapter 5 expands this into *Transformational Conversations,* a distinct theological approach to urban theology and theological research.

Educational Conversations
In Chapter 6, the previous discussions are developed into the formation of the domain of urban poor mission under the name of Urban Poor Missiology. Artifacts often demonstrate the emergence of a field - six personal artefacts contributing to the field are listed. The domain is differentiated from parallel urban missiology, community development and church growth fields, all of which are contributory.

In the following chapters, we examine some of the core areas of content in derivative Transformational Conversations. *Movement leadership* is the core of the degree explored in Chapter 7 In Chapter 8 the area of *social entrepreneurship* is expanded, and *urban spirituality* in Chapter 9.

Infrastructure Conversations
In Chapter 9 we explore *Vocational*

training Models and in Chapter 11, we switch to the mass multiplication of the domain through *Grassroots Learning Networks* that rapidly multiply the diverse content of the discipline through trainers and clusters at the grassroots. A section by Dr Hruda Lahora Ranjan demonstrates this for the Indian context.

In Chapter 11, We explore innovative technology as a significant vehicle for the multiplication at both the academic level and the grassroots. This includes a report on an experiment with cell-phone based delivery of a course.

Chapter 12, is an exploration of the *Vertical Integration of Delivery* of the domain from grassroots to doctorate. In Chapter 13 and 14, elements of platforms to expand this are reviewed.

Conclusions: Action Steps
Chapter 15 is an integration of the research in this paper into a Proposal for *Expanding the Urban Poor Leaders*

Training Commission. This includes pathways to four levels of delivery and credits and becoming an *industry professional association* with diversified funding.

Chapter 16 looks beyond, into the final goal, the transformation of oppression in the city by expansion from a Masters for slum leaders to a parallel master's for city leadership, perhaps classed as a doctorate in *Public Policy and Religion* or a *Doctorate in Transformational Urban Leadership*.

$\mathcal{A}$cknowledgements

The process of activism, and of research and writing are collective. Much in this document represents shared thinking and discussions within the *Encarnação Alliance Training Commission*, a band of activist academics, who live and work in the slums or among the poor while maintaining academic reflective practices.

Manila slum by water, CC0

Most of these leaders in the *Encarnação Alliance Training Commission* are mentioned in Chapter 2. Other leaders I have worked with through the years are mentioned in chapter 1. The best way to acknowledge them is in identifying some small part of their contribution in those chapters, though I could write a glowing chapter on each man an woman of God who shares this commitment to both the poor and to action-based theological development.

There are many- at least a hundred dear friends not mentioned; leaders of the missions founded, colaborers in church-planting, mentors, academics. If I mention one, I will offend another. For example, Bob Moffitt has modelled global patterns of see oproject based community development, Will Niewoehner has stood out as man of deep integrity over these decades in the formation of *Servant-Partners,* Craig Greenfield has multiplied patterns of caring for orphans to 10,000 children. Bobby Gupta, President of *Hindustan Bible Institute* has welcomed and supported the formation of the MATUL, encouraging at each step, Neander Kraul of *Seminario Betel* in Rio de Janeiro, has explored these ideas over many years, though we continue to wait for the right faculty to pioneer the MATUL as a *Lato Senso* (a specific Brazilian type of master's level degree) there. Scott Bessenecker has been instrumental in integrating the *New Friars,* a significant cluster of US urban poor mission leaders as he has helped scores of students explore a calling to the urban poor.

I have appreciated the liberty given me by Azusa Pacific University over the last two years to spend time in writing each semester, while they have been determining how to relaunch the international MATUL program. It is a sign of institutional grace.

My wife, Ieda, godly chaplain among cancer sufferers, preacher, lady of wisdom, has been long-suffering to allow me six weeks of concentrated time to write this. For three weeks she was with her mother in Brazil, so I used the time alone well, but when I am writing I am, as she occasionally mentions, not really present. She has given me much grace over many years. And my three adult kids, Monique, the political organizer, Leonardo, the story-teller and Bianca the interior designer have tracked various phases of development, querying or wondering, or outthinking me at each step.

Chapter 1 is based on material first published in *Living Mission.*[1] Chapter 2 is built from material in the *MATUL Commission Common Understandings.*[2] The section on *Jesus Seminary in the Slums* in chapter 3 has been published online at www.urbanleaders.org/ma since 2004. Chapter 5 is a further revision of a document first published in our book on *Developing an Auckland Business Theology*[3] - first developed with my students at New Covenant Bible College in Auckland, then published in the *PCBC Journal* for Australasian Bible Colleges, then as chapter 2 of *The Spirit of Christ and Postmodern Cities* (Grigg, 2009).

Chapter 6 on developing the domain of *Urban Poor Missiology* was forced upon me by the university wishing me to develop a portfolio about my history that demonstrates I am a credible professor, so if it is a little personal, forgive me. I have tried to rewrite it from the collective perspective as no man stands alone. It can be found on the www.urbanleaders.org/Portfolio.htm

The report of Cell-Phone Delivery was originally a Creative Teaching Grant report funded by an APU Creative Teaching grant..[4]

Dr Hruda Lahora, Dean at Mission India Theological Seminary and a significant member of the *Encarnação Alliance Training Commission*, contributed the excellent section on Grassroots Training in India.

Movement Leadership material has been online for over a decade at www.urbanleaders.org/620Leadership. Church-planting and Community Economic courses are also on the www.urbanleaders.org site.

As the pace of the movements picks up, I find I need to publish more rapidly. So this is a quick and ready document. I trust that in some future time I can revise it to something acceptable or one of my colaborers sees fit to upgrade it. It is offered as simple service to those who have sacrificed much in extending the Kingdom.

*S*pirit-directed Educational Innovation

We begin in the next chapter, with the breath of God calling these things into being. Then explore the work of the Spirit of wisdom in the mid chapters, leading us to seek the work of the Father in structuring these elements of the Spirit of creation in the latter part of the book.

For I know that whatever God does endures. Nothing can be added to it, or taken from it. God has made it that way, that mankind, should fear before him (Ecc 3:14)

The Wisdom of Aging Poverty. Photo: Max Pixel Creative Commons Zero - CC0

01
Following the Urban Spirit

Personal Reflections

Now the earth was formless and empty darkness was over the surface of the deep, and the Spirit of God was hovering over the surface of the waters...and God said...and it was so

The First Transformation, Genesis 1:2-3,7

The Spirit hovered over the chaos and formed structure in the beginning. Then at the end of the eternal drama lies the Spirit-filled city of God. The garden is in the city. He is an urbanizing God.

Over forty years ago, as an emaciated university graduate cum missionary, I recall the breath of God's Spirit infiltrating a slum, then slums, then cities of slums, and bringing transformation. In those carefree days of youth, through a few of us, the breath began as they preached the word. People were changed in Spirit-filled worship. I remember the days of healing and the deaconesses roaming and serving. I recall God's life-giving breath through young graduate professionals learning about economic development and transforming the slums. I remember friends who were defending the oppressed and the first churches that were forming in Manila's slums in the late 1970s.

That Voice and Spirit of creation continues crying out, creating order in the chaotic pain of today's mega-cities, through individuals and through a new wineskin. And the Voice perhaps calls you to be filled with that Spirit and to become that voice in the world's desperate places.

A great chaos has embraced the earth as the wealthy have legalized rights to the earth's lands. They have excluded a few billion to be landless and to migrate into that chaotic in-between known as slums— a reality between the orderliness of peasant and tribal community and the order of the urban corporate existence. It is a state of uncertain dispossession

In the last decade, one billion people, many with chickens under their feet, have careened in overloaded buses from the rural areas to the new mega-cities. They are setting up illegal shacks wherever they can find space. China alone is creating one thousand new cities this decade because of this migration. This rapid urbanization has progressed much faster than industrialization; thus most of the migrant slum dwellers live without civic infrastructure and remain underemployed or unemployed. This has created an environment of disorganization and moral and cultural disintegration.

Over time these new urban poor find footholds in the city, and gradually these slums regularize into thriving communities— if governments find a way of legalizing them, that is. Mostly they continue as places of ongoing alcoholism, violence and crime. Twenty-five years after their formation come waves of street children, and behind them waves of gangs and HIV/ AIDS-infected individuals.

It is for these responsive, dispossessed and oppressed poor that Jesus came to preach the good news. It is among them that he lived. It seems we should follow his command and do the same. He calls us to mission: wherever the gospel mission goes, people are set free from sin, and poverty begins to change as new economic communities form. When missional churches among the poor grow, injustices are addressed and communities are transformed. The good news brings justice (Is 42:1-4).

Over time these new urban poor find footholds in the city, and gradually these slums regularize into thriving communities— if governments find a way of legalizing them.

The 1980's: The Voice Calling, Birthing

One day in 1980, when I was in my little slum house in Tatalon, Manila, the same Voice of mission called, as clearly as the voice of a child: Go up the river and preach. And like Philip, I went wandering, preaching, casting out demons—I had never done that before!—and caring for a drug addict. I went, seeing what God would do next.

And again one day, a Voice over coffee as I looked out my squatter window at the higgledy-piggledy panoply of galvanized iron beneath: Go, disciple the elites at the University of the Philippines. They will change the poverty. I refused at first, for I was called to the poor, you see. But eventually I went, and invited the elites to enjoy the hospitality of the poor. Years later, I have seen hundreds of works transforming poverty, transforming structures—many from the hands of these highly educated disciples.

Yet again, in the quiet of a squatter hut during the hours of siesta prayer, I heard the Voice; this time from reading the history of missions, for God's Voice is heard in history. I could see pictures of bands of men and women, wandering Franciscan preachers. The pictures became the basis of a document for an order, *The Lifestyle and Values of Servants*, and within it, a priority

for proclamation and mobility to evangelise among the poor.

As the sun beat its hundred-degree heat onto the iron roof of that squatter home in 1980, I meditated on the life of St. Francis Xavier, apostle to the poor of India, and the life of St. Francis of Assisi. It was then that the Spirit revealed to me the centrality of incarnation, communal decision making, apostolic mobility and suffering with the poor.

Devastated by sickness and failure to combat demonic attacks, I waited on God in a forest back in New Zealand. The quiet Voice spoke "to call the church to the poor, to write the vision down". As I wandered on a 125 cc motorbike, I found a church in national revival, waiting to obey. *Companion to the Poor*, prayed into being by seventy intercessors as I wrote, touched many. *Servants to Asia's Urban Poor* exploded into life as a network of communities living in the slums and catalyzing indigenous church movements. Other missions followed in the United States and then Brazil, each through hearing his subtle nudges.

History's Echoing Voice

I was surprised by the sound of a confirming Voice a few years later in 1985, as I sat under Dr. Paul Pierson's teaching at Fuller Seminary when he taught on the history of the Celtic and Catholic orders. From this experience I wrote two seminal papers that Pierson used with other students.[5] Around that time the creative artist, John Hayes, was also captivated by the scholarship of Paul Pierson, and he pioneered *InnerCHANGE*. Movements begin with creative women and men like John, who hear the Voice and, with foolish abandon, seek to translate word into action. They are followed by dedicated fanatics who figure out how to turn the new vision and new wineskin into reality. Capable administrators then harmonize and standardize the vision and the wineskin.

An order is a network of committed communities with common values, direction and accountability between leaders. An apostolic order clearly sees the mandate Jesus gave to the apostles to go and preach. Ralph Winter was right in his 1976 analysis of structural similarities between the mobile Protestant missions and the mobile Catholic orders. But as I mused upon the question of why Protestants were not in the slums, I realized Winter had missed some central elements. At their core, the Catholic orders are distinctly different from Protestant missions. People enter Catholic communities to find God through engagement with the poor, intercession, proclamation, community and the pursuit of spiritual wisdom. It is from these that their work springs. Mother Teresa's sisters pray six hours and work five hours. Protestants, by contrast, enter mission "teams," not communities, and then they "work" or found "works" as if they were starting a business.

While living in the slums and wondering why Protestants had failed

among the poor, I realized that we must first establish caring communities, not work teams, for the human costs are high. And we must primarily become seekers of God instead of founders of works, for work will not sustain us through the traumas of incarnation. We formed Servants as a movement with aims of seeking God through rapid proclamation among the poor and multiplication of indigenous movements of churches based on a lifestyle of incarnation, community, simplicity, suffering and sacrifice.

The 1990's: The Voice, & Indigenous Urban Poor Missions

In response to prayer in 1988, while I was living in a *favela* in Brazil, God touched a gracious apostolic leader, Pastor Waldemar Carvalho, and *Kairos* was formed. Kairos is a Brazilian mission community, multiplying works and denominations in a dozen cities. There was little talk about values and orders but Kairos closely matched the narrowly focused

nature of the early Wesleyan circuit preachers, who emulated the early Franciscan preachers, who in turn had learned from the preaching Lollards.

We dreamed together of Latin Americans in the slums of Kolkata. I believe Kairos was the first truly indigenous Brazilian mission community, and it is now one of the biggest, calling people from the slums to the slums and not dependent on the West. Each worker lives on about three hundred dollars per month in community houses so they can pool their money. They suffer greatly as they pioneer slum churches. Kairos established a denomination with a Bible school in Lima, Peru, then in Mexico and then in Africa and China. They started a new denomination in Bangladesh and established soccer clubs (what else would Brazilians do?) for street kids in Kolkata.

The apostolic workers of *Kairos* come from both Pentecostal and mainline churches, balancing the power of the Spirit and of intellectualism, as middle-class people and poor people serving

Come Holy Spirit, Art4TheGlryOfGod by Sharon, CC0

together. In the West we would call them communities, but to Brazilians this is just normal extended family dynamics. "What is all this talk about community as a value?" Brazilians ask; for them, it is simply how one does life.

For ten years I sojourned in and out of Kolkata with my Brazilian wife, spending three or six months at a time, to prepare the ground for the coming of *Kairos* there. Our workers experienced a struggle so grotesque that few of those who have become part of the vision can talk of it. It is a city in which only intercessors survive, in which every worker is damaged by the evil one. It is a story in which workers lost their hearing and their emotional health, in which demonic attacks were so devious that they beggar description and in which only intense prayer moved officials to place a stamp in a passport. The struggle over those years resulted in the first church in the Kolkata slums, and then fifteen cell groups. These were planted through the work of a simple Bengali disciple and his wife, a healer.

I share some of these instances of pain and hardship to say that our call, in these next decades before the King returns, must be to these most difficult cities. And transformation will not come without intercessory communities entering these cities first. The preaching orders of the twelfth to sixteenth centuries were often partners with an intercessory order of women. We need to see equivalent twenty-first-century orders of intercessors connected to these workers among the poor; in Kolkata we urged every worker to garner seven hundred intercessors just to survive spiritually.

We began to multiply storytelling consultations of slum pastors in cities. I knew from my teen years reading hundreds of missions biographies, that real apostolic speed is not going to happen predominantly with Western workers, although without them/us, many who are needed to catalyze movements to the poor would be missing. Apostolic speed will happen with indigenous leaders, many of them born and raised in the slums and leading bands of men and women into other slums.

Rongsenmeren Jamir, for instance, was from Nagaland, a state of India that had experienced revival but that for decades has been brutalized by the Indian army. He was a pastor of a three-thousand member church. Touched one day by this call to live among the poor, he left his position to pursue life among the poor and discovered migrant workers living in a quarry. He began a small church, then five churches, now seventy-five. Within a year, he had begun training twenty missionaries from Nagaland for the slums of India, forming a new mission, *Justice for the Poor*. Incarnation, or living with the people we serve, is a critical sign. Evangelizing and establishing churches is a critical focus. Working together with our poor friends to find solutions to the

economic and social needs is an essential aspect of pastoral care. Rongsenmeren devoted himself to these things.

Some of his workers joined a couple in Kolkata to learn how to train women in tailoring. This couple did not preach but, in a most beautiful way, kept on loving and helping until the women asked them about their Lord. Soon the whole group of women tailors from the slums were starting every day with worship and Bible study. When they graduated from training in dressmaking, they set up their own businesses that employed others. Thus *economic discipleship* continued to multiply hand in hand with spiritual transformation. This is inherent in true spirituality.

In the twenty-five years since writing about socio-economic-spiritual discipleship in *Companion to the Poor*, I have walked with scores of slum pastor friends as we have kept expanding ways of implementing these kingdom economic principles. Discipleship is our response to the King and his kingdom. Economic discipleship involves those parts of our lives related to the material world, our living out of what we have come to teach as ten economic discipleship principles: human dignity; creativity; productivity; cooperative economics; work and rest; detachment and simplicity; redistribution for equality; management, savings and debt; celebration and land ownership.

Some of the missional practices that indigenous workers develop are markedly different from those of majority-world apostolic orders moving into the slums (who are mostly wealthy, middle-class, educated people). The emergent, majority-world missions that rise from among the poor don't, for instance, like the word order, and they would never use the word friar. My task of bringing unity has often involved bridging incarnational works like *Kairos* which are being stirred up from among the poor, with those incarnational works emerging from the West.

Generally, churches come first, becoming economic communities. Sometimes kingdom economics comes first and then leads to gospel proclamation and to church planting. This is illustrated in the work of a dynamic business professor in Manila, who started five thousand micro-enterprise projects among the poor. One day, when challenged that her ministry was not holistic because the gospel

was not being presented, she shifted and set out to establish five thousand Bible studies, out of which have come three hundred churches.

The Kingdom is spiritual and economic, and in the eyes of our majority-world brothers and sisters living and working among the poor, the kingdom cannot come without the multiplication of churches. Western incarnational workers tend to talk more of mission as justice, because poverty immediately forces us to deal with our wealth. Wealthy people talk of programs and projects, which require money.

2000's: Postmodern Learning Networks

In the early 2000's, we gathered leaders of both Western and non-Western incarnational movements and orders into the *Encarnação Alliance of Urban Poor Movement Leaders*. At our gathering in Bangkok in 2004, God spoke through a prophet of the need for fifty thousand workers from the slums to the slums. All said "Amen!" So this became a goal that we would strive for, with God's help. As part of this we developed training modules on CDs and have been multiply-

Grassroots Training of Church-planters, Chennai, India.

ing this curriculum city by city through "city learning networks." This has resulted in many new churches.

One day after the Bangkok gathering, I prayed and heard the Voice again. *Go to Africa,* it said. *I will provide.* Go, find a cluster of pastors in the slums and train them. I asked God to show me someone under the radar. Then, while searching online for references to revival, I noticed an obscure website about a slum pastor's library. As I read the words on the site, I was overwhelmed by the presence of the Spirit. Here was a pastor in the slums, seeking to train others with a library! What days of sweet fellowship I was soon enjoying with slum pastors of Uganda. How intense the debate between them as to whether kingdom economics was from God. From that time together, a network of missional Ugandan slum pastors emerged. They have formed three new clusters of churches in three countries. AIDS victims have been cared for, and small micro-enterprise projects have begun.

A few years ago, when I was back in my home country of New Zealand, the Voice spoke again. This time it said: *Go train in India. I will provide.* An email from India came the next day, asking for training. Out of that venture one hundred pastors were trained, and God has indeed provided, multiplying that first training experience ten times over. Slum pastors are now being trained in eighteen different Indian cities (and as I write, another series in another city is happening). Many new churches have been planted, lepers have been reached, widows have been cared for, gypsies and orphans have been loved and women have been trained in sewing.

The Millennial Future: Empowerment of Cross and Resurrection

So here is the call: to ferment movements of the Spirit created through four phases of empowerment. First there is the *dunamis* of the preached word of God (which is the power of the gospel according to Romans 1:16); then the liberating life of the Spirit, which comes through conversion; then the growth of God-communities of faith expressed in social, spiritual, economic, political and environmental discipleship. These three lead to a fourth phase of broader cultural engagement and transformation: derivative works, such as community organizations, development projects, urban planning and health programs, which are all initiated by and infused with the Holy Spirit. Many more people are needed to walk alongside slum leaders— first to learn and then to facilitate, according to one's gifts, the various aspects of these four empowerments.

Lest you put on rose-tinted glasses, remember that along with these great blessings, we must be prepared to live with great pain, daily carrying in our bodies the real cost of the cross. There is daily sickness. There can be hidden costs for children of workers among the poor who are always on the move; at times they become traumatized teenagers. There are unknown costs to some of our spouses as well, who may complain very little but inwardly struggle with the immense pressures of homelessness, chaos and deep loneliness. There is grief at the loss of workers—a brother pulls back from a critical work when his health fails; a demonic attack proves too much for another; all of us are tripped up by hidden sins. It would be more graphic to tell you the actual stories, but I can't, since some of these involve living people.

The Spirit, Humility and Greater Works

Preaching friars? Apostolic orders? These are my reflections on more than forty years of Spirit-freedom, apostolic mobility and transformation. Despite our frailties and through many failures, as bands of brothers and sisters among the poor, we have now seen these orders multiply to hundreds of workers and indigenous movements multiply to many thousands.

The daughter works are reaching hundreds of thousands. Whatever God does endures forever; nothing can be added to it or taken from it (Eccles 3:14). God is the source, and God will determine the ending point of a given new mission or a new wineskin. God alone is to be praised!

I invite you to come and catch the wind! Come! Dance and run with us as we speed the message of the cross. You may not be perfect, you may not be brilliantly gifted, you may not know what God would do through you, but his voice will lead you, his presence will be with you and the joy of your children walking in truth will sustain you. Come, walk with us as we follow Jesus, the Voice.

The next chapter will lead us more deeply into the pathways of the Spirit in launching training for slum leaders globally. This chapter has been of the Spirit as the divine wind, the next is of seeking the Spirit as Isaiah (11:2), portrays her, the Spirit of wisdom and knowledge, counsel and understanding.

Upgraded Heliopolis, 1996

Vlv Grigg, home in Heliopolis favela, Sao Paulo, Brazil, 1988

02

Pathways to Seminaries in the Slums

It began in a small cloud in a sky, above Ateneo Park in Manila in 1976. I was 25. My first church-planting team were spending the day together seeking the Lord as to how we should plant the church in Kamuning. I looked up and heard a voice as clear as day, "Unless you create a master's' degree for slum leaders where they have space to think, they will die". That was it. Nothing fancy. No design. No structure. Just a command. I saw, as clearly as one sees a cloud in a still sky, that movements among the poor would not eventuate without the training of movement leaders at a master's-degree level.

"He will guide you into all truth" (John 16:13).

It would take us 20 years to work out how to do it!

First we had to live it. To pay the same price that workers in the slums pay. To struggle with all the issues from how to enter, to how to preach, to how to form churches. Leadership was yet a bigger challenge. And how to engage in the complexity of social, economic and political issues.

Then years of recruiting workers, relocating them, training them and learning from them as we formed global and indigenous missions. All the time, thinking, writing, studying.

It wasn't until thirty years later that the *Encarnação Training Commission* in a shared wonderful sense of unity around this vision of master's-level training launched the *MA in Transformational Urban Leadership*. Initially in three schools.

Genesis of the Program

Following story-telling consultations of urban poor leaders in Mumbai (93) and Hong Kong (96), the *Encarnação Alliance Consultation* of urban poor mission leaders in Sao Paulo in 2002 concluded that collectively we should develop our own training processes for urban poor workers.

At the *Encarnação Alliance Consultation* in Bangkok in July 2004, we sensed that the Lord was in process of mobilising 50,000 to the slums of Asia, Africa and South America of indigenous and cross cultural new workers to meet the need of deepening poverty, growing migrant populations from rural contexts, and the responsiveness of the urban poor.

New urban poor holistic church planting movements that are deeply involved in holistic ministry and implementing income-generating projects that would result in viable communities of believers are desperately needed. These movements are catalyzed by those who live an incarnation lifestyle among the urban poor. The fastest growing of these

Home, Tatalon, Manila

movements flourish where healing and deliverance are normal aspects of church life.

The delegates at the July, 2004 Consultation in Bangkok identified three levels of training and equipping needed in urban poor ministry:

1. **Grass Roots Training:** Existing workers are to be trained in a storytelling model of training teams of new workers.

This has been delivered to 3000+ leaders in 27 cities and been developed around 12 course modules available on CD, covering 40 topic areas. The modules include: Introduction for Trainers; Spiritual Formation; Theological Framework for Slum Ministry; Slum Context; Slum Evangelism; Discipleship of the Urban Poor; Church Growth in the Slums; Leadership Among the Urban Poor; Kingdom and Transformational Development; Urban Poor Mission Structures; Kingdom and Land Rights Conflicts; and an integration module. Brian Johnson continued to develop this for some years.

2. **Undergraduate Degree (BA) in Theology of Urban Ministry:** The Encarnação Alliance members saw this as an expansion of the grassroots courses with diplomas into a formal degree structure for equipping existing workers who have had no formal education but several years of ministry experience, or business people who have been assisting urban poor ministry teams on a part-time basis and are now considering full-time service.

3. **Graduate Degree in Urban Leadership.** Potential students were identified as either:
•Existing workers with a number years experience and proven leadership ability to be prepared for future apostolic roles to give leadership.
• Those with pastoral ministry experience who sense the call of God to the urban poor and desire to multiply urban poor ministries through team building.
•Those with the call of God to the poor having a strong sense of injustice and wanting to use business experience to economically liberate the poor.
•Movement pioneers who would catalyse new movements among the urban poor in targeted slums in the poorest countries of the world.
(These outcomes have since been reworked).

Implementation

From 2002, I visited 13 seminaries with these ideas, constantly refining a list of 433 outcomes indicated by church-planters and development workers from 22 consultations in cities,[6] and from this an initial program design of 23 courses. Bryan Johnson worked with me in putting the initial course descriptions together.

From 20 years of discussing some of these needs with schools, even though it is essentially core theology I determined that this should be a leadership program by definition, as against a theological program (which would immediately invoke the addition of 7-9 core courses). This would defuse opposition from the traditional theological faculty, and minimise friction as the new style of theologising took root. I had used the *Transformational Conversations* model of doing theology with urban students and in citywide consultations for a number of years.

In Nairobi, Colin Smith had developed similar ideas in moving a training school based at Carlile College into the slum of Kibera and launching a BA degree. At three other institutions there was an immediate sense of compatibility and the MA program was launched at Asian Theological Seminary in Manila (July 2007), Hindustan Bible Institute in Chennai (July, 2007) and Azusa Pacific University in LA (Jan 2010). Rich Slimbach of APU brilliantly took the initial program design and simplified it down into a Program Proposal which we used as a basis for consensus between the schools. Throughout this time, Viv raised funding for travel and coordination costs from donors and some foundations.

Program Directors from these schools were invited into the *Encarnação Alliance Commission* which met in Chennai, Nov 2006, and they, plus selected faculty, then met in Bangkok, Feb 2007, to work on course design processes that would enable input and ownership by the Indian and Filipino faculties so this at the outset was a degree from the coal face. Corrie de Boer functioned as chair of the commission. Lee Wanak was appointed program director in Manila and he and Corrie de Boer recruited adjunct faculty along with some existing faculty to do the course design and delivery. Paul Cornelius was appointed principal at HBI and recruited two faculty to develop this. Faculty continued to work on these course designs through to the end of 2008.

Dr Corrie de Boer became vice chair and Dr Viv Grigg moved from coordinator to chairperson, with the coordinator's role left vacant during the economic downturn. Viv moved from New Zealand to APU in Los Angeles in 2010 to direct the APU launch, while Dr Rich Slimbach continued on as Academic Director in his overload time. Dr Peter Nitschke took over

Two Year Full Time Option

TUL	FALL		SPRING		SUMMER
500	Biblical Theology of Urban Mission	560	Theology & Practice of Community Economics	505	Language and Culture Acquisition II
520	Urban Spirituality	505	Language and Culture Acquisition I	630	Community Transformation
550	Forming New Faith Communities	650	Primary Health Care		
			Year 2		
555	Educational Centre Development	620	Leadership in Urban Movements	640	Entrepreneurial & Organizational Leadership
540	Urban Reality and Theology	555	Educational Centre Development	655	Advocacy and the Urban Environment
530	Service to the Marginalized	670	Qualitative & Urban Research Methods	670	Research Project

from Dr Lee Wanak in 2011 at ATS, and Dr Saravanan became program director at HBI in 2008. Dr Colin Smith launched the MATUL at Carlile in partnership with St Paul's University in 2011, and Mission India Theological School launched that year also under Dr Hruda Lahora Ranjan, the Dean. In 2013, The Dean of the School of Theology, Dr Olivia Nassaka and Rev Dr David Andrew Omana hosted the Commission at Uganda Christian University. In 2015, a gathering was held in Manila at ATS.

At the 2010 meeting of the Commission, there was a sense that Colin Smith should seek the Lord for five schools in Africa, Saravanan for five in India, and Corrie de Boer was assigned this role in South East Asia. The Lord began to speak to leaders in various partner schools in Accra, Kampala, Addis Ababa. *Seminario Betel* in Rio de Janiero planned to launch in 2013 as a *Lato Senso* (a lower level Masters, less academic, in some ways equivalent to a postgraduate diploma), but the right personnel are not yet in place. Uganda Chris-

tian University launched in 2017, but is still building capacity for enough students for viability.

Institutional Frustrations

But we did not count on the inherent instability of higher educational institutions.

- Each time there is a change in president, dean, director or admin staff, the programs falter. The role of a dean is one of the most complex of any roles, and requires exceptional leaders. With exceptions, each new dean often make changes with little time or sense of need to be trained in the essential nature of the program, its underlying values or structure - just what they can see as boxes on paper. At APU, the program experienced 7 deans and associate deans in seven years, and 3 directors, with accountability to 29 different people - the people were godly, very gifted, the administrators efficient, but the institutional infrastructure a little unwieldy!!

- When financial crises hit schools, as happens usually yearly, attempts are consistently made to cut the administrative assistant - which is short-sighted, as without recruitment there is no income. Innovation within institutions is generally not welcome.

- Nor did we count on the spiritual warfare. Dr Saravanan was leading in Chennai when he had a motor cycle accident which severely incapacitated him. Dr Paul Rollet, a marathon runner, one of the early students from the US in Manila and one taking the MATUL into lower level delivery, fell down a cliff severely damaging his back.

- But the major problem has been the failure of the schools to engage with their feeder groups, the slum pastors networks. The educated classes that make up the faculty are often averse to the chaos of slum Pentecostalism. And are used to students simply showing up for traditional programs. Recruitment is not generally part of faculty job descriptions and is not extra pay, so not all are willing to take on the unpaid role of recruiters as well as faculty. A reasonably paid coordinator who can relate to the slum leaders is necessary.

Creative Expansion

Other schools have creatively diversified the initial design. HBI are now looking at an undergraduate version that feeds into an urban master's. MITS developed a non-formal delivery of that same program and integrated other courses into the MDiv, ATS developed the CTUL and created a pathway from the MATUL to MDiv. Rev. Michael Mata at APU developed a US domestic version of the program as a Community Development program based on his World Vision experience appropriate for the US context, and using a hybrid delivery system.

The next chapter looks at the courses, then explores Jesus' educational content, demonstrating how it underlies the structure of the MATUL. By contrast, it does not define the structure of an MDiv degree of traditional theology. Perhaps our style is closer to Jesus' theology? What are the implications?.

The Informal Economy

Smokey Mountain Garbage Dump, Manila. Home to many

03

Seminary in the Slums - Courses

Extended Family

Global slum culture - daily slum routines

Foundational Courses

TUL500 **A Biblical Theology of Urban Mission:** This course relates the biblical motif of the Kingdom of God to issues of leadership development in resource-poor urban communities.

TUL520 **Urban Spirituality:** An in-depth examination of human development and family life in the slum context, this course emphasizes the care and nurturing of resource-poor workers and the practical application of the spiritual disciplines.

TUL530 **Building Faith Communities:** This course applies a story-telling approach to the process of entering poor communities and developing holistic poor peoples' churches in ways faithful to the values and goals of the Kingdom of God. (Internships).

Core Action-Reflection Courses

TUL505 & 506 **Language and Culture Acquisition:** (For those moving across a culture) This course guides students in acquiring the knowledge and skills for independent language and culture learning within urban-poor communities.

TUL540 **Urban Reality and Theology:** This course aims to generate perspectives and tools for transformative urban mission.

TUL620 **Leadership in Urban Movements:** This course explores the dynamics of leadership within holistic, urban-poor movements.

TUL630 **Community Transformation:** Students explore the challenges, models of, and prospects for, transformational change within slum communities while developing a Christian framework for holistic development, organization, and advocacy among the urban poor and gaining facility in community asset mapping.

TUL640 **Entrepreneurial and Organizational Leadership:** This course introduces the concepts and skills of entrepreneurial and organizational leadership required to initiate new movement structures among the urban poor.

Social Entrepreneurship Internships(3 or 4 of 5)

TUL550 **Service to the Marginalized:** This course guides students in understanding the conditions of marginalized populations and in formulating a theology and strategy for team-based responses that aim to free individuals and change structural causes.

TUL555 **Educational Centre Development:** This course offers analysis of third world schooling with a focus on developing and improving preschool, elementary, and technical schools in the slums as integral to the work of urban poor churches.

TUL560 **Theology and Practice of Community Economics:** This course relates biblical and theological perspectives on human development to the theory and practice of community wealth building. Special emphasis is given to considering how working women in the slums might use micro-enterprises and individual development accounts to create a better environment for asset building and ownership.

TUL650 **Primary Health Care:** An exploration of public health challenges facing the Church within slum communities, along with innovative, community-based responses, this course highlights topics such as environmental health, maternal and child health, and chronic health conditions prevalent in slums. Students serve as mentored interns with a health organization in the community where they live or work.

TUL 655 **Advocacy and the Urban Environment:** Students examine the relations between urban poor communities, the land, and broader environmental problems including natural disasters. Fieldwork focuses on advocacy for adequate housing and infrastructure services.

Final Research Project

TUL670 **Qualitative Research Methods:** Students apply qualitative action-reflection, development and missiological research methods to a design of a project proposal

TUL675 **Research Project:** Students apply analytic frameworks and practical skills acquired through the program to an investigation of an issue on behalf of a community organization.

Modifications

Each school is expected to add in a systematic theology and a biblical studies course taught by the existing theological faculty. Each course is 3 units of 40-45 hours per unit, or 120-135 hours per course including theology, social analysis and action. Some schools reduce this to 39 units, some expand it to 54. Local Deans, faculty and the Commission on Higher Education or similar in that country, may all impose variations to the above. Ideally 80% remains the same so that cross-fertilization between the schools is possible. There is an expressed need to add a course on *Dealing with Violence and Reconciliation*.

MATUL Training Commission, Uganda, 2014

Jesus' Seminary in the Slums
Theological Derivation

This is our humble attempt to follow Jesus-style education in the slums, to get the seminary into the slums!!

I was in Manila at the launch of the *MA in Transformational Urban Leadership*, preaching about I Corinthians 1:9-25, and the contrast between Jesus'-style education and the education of the academe. For Jesus was an educator - a brilliant mind. He recruited learners around him.

He knew of the Greek philosophic systems that Paul rejects here, and could have taught within them. For he grew up in Nazareth, 4 miles from Sapporis, one of the leading Greek-Roman cities, where all the philosophies of the world crossed. He maybe built houses there. But he chose a different methodology for his educative process. It involved action-reflection more than philosophy, and built from the stories of the people, proverbs, and parables as these interfaced with God's story and the conundrums of the trinity.

Following Jesus in the 21st C context, this MA is an action-reflection degree built around a process I call *Transformational Conversations*, a process of discerning truth through holistic story-telling. Some academics think this is not *kosher*. That truth can only be found through Platonic logic. Jesus was smarter.

His syllabus began with 40 days of prayer and fasting, so we begin with *Urban Spirituality*. This is logical for the wisdom of Israel, was that *"the fear of the Lord is the beginning of wisdom."* This puts the MATUL outside of humanistic academia. They encounter the Holy Spirit in the cross as part of the process of spiritual formation. They experience that Spirit in liberation from sin, from trauma, from bondage to human philosophies (and false doctrines and traditions, that Paul and Jesus so opposed) and being liberated from oppressive, abusive leaders (often religious). They begin to enter into the liberty of his work ministering to others.

Then, in the power of the Spirit, he began to preach, build a team and disciple, elements of the course in *Urban Poor Church-planting*. What he preached was the Kingdom of God, so next is an overview of the scriptures, *A Biblical Theology of Urban Mission* particularly referencing the Kingdom of God, poverty, oppression, societal structures, and other issues for slum dwellers.

Of course, his declared focus was the poor. In fact, the next course is one on *Standing with the Marginalized* – prostitutes, street children, drug addicts.

He understood the issues of the day. What do you think a rebel leader like Simon the Zealot and a tax collector discussed over supper along with John, the son of one of the leading families? Jesus discussed ways of understanding the signs of the times, so a course on *Urban Realities and*

Theology helps students understand the social, economic and political context of the city and poverty through the lenses of various urban sociology, urban anthropology, urban economic and urban geography theories.

He expected his disciples to bear much fruit. *Movement Leadership* grapples with multiplication. Jesus was very engaged with the rich. In fact, Nicodemus came to him because he was caring for the poor - issues of *Advocacy and Justice* connecting rich and poor, were important to him. And he was involved in healing, caring for lepers, thus a course on *Primary Health* and Caring for HIV/AIDS victims.

A quarter of his teaching was on economics, so *Community Economics* and a course on *Entrepreneurial Management* along with developing *Slum Education*, so that every pastor can train his eldership in small business and each church can become a viable economic unit and solve the property barrier through an associated school.

Jesus mentored. All these are taught by action-reflection methods, with a balance of extensive practicum, classroom reflection and guided readings. These are integrated with mentoring by church-planters and by leaders of ministries throughout the degree in Field Education courses. Since we do have to interface with the academe (descendant of Plato), the reflection is refined in a final *Integration Project or Thesis*.

The next chapter looks at Jesus' educational principles as they are expanded in the underlying educational philosophy, or andragogy, of the MATUL.

Hindustan Bible Institute
first MATUL graduation

Training Organizations in Manila

04

Poorology: a Discussion on Andragogy, with Freire and Jesus

Jesus' Wisdom Andragogy

At the core of Jesus' andragogy was the incarnation among the people that led to gathering a band of apprentices (He chose twelve). This enabled character formation (to be with him) and the transmission of skills (to be sent out to preach) (Mark 3:14).

Thus our training must follow his approach to character formation and commitment to the centrality of proclamation.

Why is preaching so important in his educational strategy? In most oral cultures oratory is an art that is highly prized, and usually highly stylized with culturally affirmed patterns of audience response.

In African-American culture, for example, preaching is a refined art, beginning softly, with increasing tempo, and rhythm, rising to a series of crescendos then a final denouement. At each bend in the road of the argument there is great alliteration, there are repeated combinations of ideas in triplets, the audience knows the appropriate communal responses to encourage the preacher along at each points.

In Filipino preaching, usually one begins with a pithy saying, a proverb or a trick question.

Theoretical Approaches in Urban Poor Community-Based Education

Character! cohort! spiritual formation! academic foundation! face to face pastoral care! engagement with reality in context! Best practice urban missions education!!! What are some elements of the educational philosophy that underlies such a dynamic delivery system?.

The Origins of Andragogy

Pedagogy relates to education of children. Andragogy relates to Adult Education, a more common term in the English-speaking world (the Latin roots makes more sense in Portuguese, Spanish and French). In reality, Paulo Friere's *Pedagogy of the Oppressed,* that we shall explore a little later is in the field of *andragogy.* The term is credited to Malcome Knowles (1913-77).[7]

Andragogy

The adult wants to participate in the development of his own education and has a strong sense of himself (involved adult learners)

Education relates to experience with the right to make one's own mistakes (adult learners experience)

The adult want to feel the relevance of what he learns (relevant impact to learners lives)

The adult wants to learn by solving concrete and current problems instead of assimilating content. (problem –centered). (Dusan Savicevic, 1996)

Jesus also followed the way of the rabbis, with his wisdom sayings, and his argumentation that left the people amazed, as with each question he responds with a question, often one that was unanswerable. His teaching is scattered with jokes and double meanings. He hides ideas in plain site from those who will not hear. He leaves people with a demand to obey, but it is open: "Let him who has ears hear", a demand that allows for reflection and time, yet requires action based on the new idea. All of this constantly creating an alternative reality to the existing realities in which they dwelt.

Freire: Problem Solving Education

Brazilian educational philosopher, Paulo Freire, is well-known in educational circles. Some estimate that 2 million educators around the world work with his theoretical framework. His seminal work, *Pedagogy of the Oppressed* (1996), sets a standard for education among the urban poor. He developed his theories from working among peasant labourers in te poorest area of the North East of Brazil and identifying the culture of silence in context of paternalism and oppression. He identified the education system as one of the major instruments for the maintenance of this culture of silence.

Some of his significant ideas:

His philosophy centres around *conscientizacao*, whereby the oppressed recognize the causes of their oppression, so that through transformative action, they can create a new situation.

Education is not a banking system where deposits of info are made to people

deficit with knowledge, but the knowledge lies in the adult learners and in their understanding of complex contexts (in our case, Americans have little knowledge of the overseas urban poor context, so we are forced to draw on knowledge from leaders on the field)

Problem-solving education is a process towards *conscientizacao*.

The educator is a facilitator to draw out this knowledge and link it to globalized concepts.

> *Authentic education is not carried on by "A" for "B" or by "A about "B", but rather by "A" with "B"* (Freire 1998:76).

> *When teachers implement problem-solving education in the classroom, the approach students as fellow dialoguers, which creates an atmosphere of hope, love, humility, trust* (1998:72).

Action Learning Outcomes: Learning is for purpose of action, and transformation of oppressive situations.

Identity is developed through processing responses to oppression - this is a cooperative learning approach.

Democratic/Freedom-Based Education

Freire's approach is not the only basis for this style of education as liberation. The same theme is also framed within the American ideal of democracy.

This is a Christian belief underlying the Reformation and foundational to the Puritan villages which were the bedrock to birthing the concepts of American education as the settlers, Puritans from England, Huegenots from France, Mennonites, Amish and Pietists from Germany, all sought to escape the oppression of Europe and gain freedom and equality in a new land. The underlying commitment of the Reformation to the dignity of the individual, all being equal before God, has educational corollaries. Ability to study the scriptures, and civic engagement both require an education preparing some for:

- Ethical living in their community and profession.
- Civic leadership in their community: social, political, economic, spiritual.
- Wider national civic leadership.
- Women also are equal before God, so education is for both men and women.

Education as the practice of freedom - as opposed to education as the practice of domination - denies that man is abstract, isolated, independent, and unattached to this world; it also denies that the world exists as a reality apart from the people. Authentic reflection considers neither abstract man nor the world without people, but people in relations with the world. (Freire, 1998: 81).

Democratic/ freedom-based education is grounded in the premise that people are naturally curious and have an innate desire to learn and grow. If left unfettered, un-coerced, and un-manipulated (i.e.. by conventional educational practices that often result in the diminishment of these innate characteristics), people will vigorously and with gusto pursue their interests, and thus learn and make meaning on their own and in concert with others. And because these individuals are honoured and respected in this process, they become socialized to honour and respect the dignity and autonomy of others.

A master's' degree is independent research in the English or European world. After experience of fostering research-based graduate education in my classes in the English-education world, I was aghast at the regimentation required within the online delivery framework of my U.S. University, and the expectation of Master's students, that they would continue being structured every week with forum, assignments, readings into machine-like learning dictated by the professor. I have some experience in organisational systems design, so mused that I can not buck a system even if it has extended high-school type didactics into master's - level structure following a Behaviourist model, but perhaps I could shift it towards the higher levels of constructivist best practice.

Thus, applying a Freirean/democratic process, students became involved each year in the design and evalua-

tion of the MATUL program. Some courses we were able to start with a clean slate as they involved topics where there was no previous field of knowledge, so we created them together – land rights, community economics in the slums, urban poor church-planting, slum movement leadership. Professors guided them with the issues, and some initial frameworks. They fleshed these out with local knowledge and local literature. We supplemented that with experience and global literature. The learning was less in the content as in the process of discovering the content, the "aha" moments that occurred weekly as reports of action from 8 cities around the globe came in, with supporting literature from within the culture! Collectively-owned!

Take the global struggles for land rights for example. To begin with, no student knew what the issues really were of dispossession. Nor how the laws functioned. Nor how the NGO's that were interning with engaged. Nor how Islamic or Hindu thinking affected concepts of justice, let alone Christian perspectives on advocacy.

By the end of that class (the only one in the world connecting theology and practice of land rights that I can find), they were sufficiently expert as to be able to discuss with any NGO leader the processes, the issues, the structures needed.

And *they* did it, I was just "one of the group", quietly assisting them to design, directing to sources, integrating the ideas. And, at times, teaching as the expert theologian and practitioner - it is not all student-driven.

One could do that with face-to-face synchronous weekly online classrooms. It would not have been possible with the asynchronous and high transactional distance delivery that had been developed fifteen years ago and now was being perfected across the university in preparation for roboticization of online learning.

*I*nfluences on Freire

The spiritual roots of Freire were significant.[8] There is deep commitment to the incarnation or solidarity with the poor that has marked many Catholic educational orders. Liberation theology was also prominent, that had prioritized social justice and political activism, These were Jesuit Catholic themes. This emphasis also rejected the hierarchical nature of the church and sought to form base communities around a political understanding of conscientization. The diffusion of power is something as Protestants we have fought for for hundreds of years. The imposition of Marxist analysis in the liberation theology that was popular among Catholic intellectuals of his time is one that does not continue to carry weight as Marx's analysis is no longer valid in a multipolar world and his solutions proven to be disastrous globally.

The warm humanity of Freire perhaps stems from his early family and school experiences. His educational framework begins with Teixeira, who called for the democratization of Brazilian society through education.[9] This, Teixeira learned as a student of John Dewey. From Dewey he also imbibed the idea that the student learns through active involvement, instead of being a passive receiver of knowledge, and that the ideal teacher would be open-minded and confident in their competence but open to learning and sharing with his or her students.

From the psychologist philosopher, Erich Fromm, came his critical pedagogy concepts in his *Escape from Freedom* (1983). He advocated the creation of human values, instead of following pre-existing norms.

More complex were his understanding of the radical left-wing, though he later in life was consistent in his not being a radical but seeking incremental change. The Algerian, Frantz Fanon (*The Wretched of the Earth* (1963)), helped Freire make sense of the colonization experience. The Brazilian oppression was deeper than class consciousness. Fanon, the left-wing activist, believed that the oppressed must be actively engaged at every step of gaining their freedom. Antonio Gramsci's idea of the organic intellectual from within the community, who could best transform the community became significant (1982). To Gramsci, it was the duty of organic intellectuals to speak to the obscured precepts of folk wisdom, or common sense (senso comune), of their respective politic spheres. These intellectuals would represent excluded social groups of a society, and articulate, through the language of culture, the feelings and experiences which the masses could not express for themselves.

Critical Pedagogy

From Freire, another educational philosophy and social movement theory has become popular in aca-

Freire is within the Educational Field of Constructivism i.e. Learning involves active engagement with social change

Constructivism

- learners are actively involved in a process of knowledge construction vs. passively receiving information.

Derived from Pragmatism

John Dewey

Jean Piaget

Deconstructivism (Illich)

Freire: conscientization: education as a vehicle of the poor engaging oppression

Lev Vigotsky (social reconstructivism)

demic circles. Advocates of *critical pedagogy* view teaching as an inherently political act, reject the neutrality of knowledge, and insist that issues of social justice and democracy itself are not distinct from acts of teaching and learning.

The goal of critical pedagogy is emancipation from oppression through an awakening of the critical consciousness, based on the Portuguese term *conscientização*. When achieved, critical consciousness encourages individuals to effect change in their world through social critique and political action. This can be seen to extend Freire into the philosophic domain.

Peter McLaren, a leading voice in this intellectual movement identifies six steps in problem-solving education.
1. Students and teachers approach their acts of knowing as grounded in individual experience
2. They approach the historical and cultural world as transformable reality shaped by human ideological representations of reality
3. Learners make connections between their own conditions and the conditions produced through the making of reality.
4. They consider ways they can shape this new reality This is collective
5. They develop skills to put their ideas into print, giving power to the act of knowing.
6. They identify the myths of domination discourse and work to destabilize these myths, ending the cycle of oppression. (McLaren, 1999:51)

Jane Vela: Dialogical Adult Education

Jane Vela (2002), a disciple of Freire, working in Africa among the poor, similarly builds on the idea of Conversations. Adults learn best through a "dialogue" that takes place in an atmosphere of mutual respect and safety, and with learning designs that are grounded in the reality of their lives. Thus contextual education is a significant principle.

Grigg: Transformational Conversations

Paulo Freire CC0

Over 30 years I have been developing a new urban missions theology paradigm entitled Transformational Conversations that begin with the motivation of entrance stories into poverty that shock people into seeking Biblical answers. These result in engaging in a theological conversation. At the same time they need to be fed by the city conversation, the socio-economic or political conversation. The result is a new conversation that seeks transformation. This is usually outworked in urban structures that are an outworking of an urban theology in praxis. This will be expanded in the next chapter

Training students in such processes requires constant conversations as they engage in their communities. The very manner of learning is conversational not didactic.

Transformational Conversations: a More Comprehensive Approach
This continues Freire's commitment to the location of education among the oppressed. While it involves affirmation of the perceptions of the oppressed, also engages in liberation from oppression trauma through spirituality, and social engagement with liberation from socio-economic oppression through analysis that results in action. Oppression is not viewed as primarily political, but is at its roots spiritual - expressed at times through political dynamics, social dynamics, family dynamics, personal experiences of violation, class

distinctions and barriers. All find liberation through the expression of Christ the healer and reconciler in the cultural domain, the political domain, the social domain, the personal domain. He is all in all.

Socio-economic-political analysis identifies the cause of trauma. Theological reflection identifies the nature of Christ in response – in the proclamation of repentance, prayer, community development, community organization, creation of businesses, social movements. Each can be an expression of the Christ who infuses all structures, all in all.

Transformational Conversations as a Research Methodology

This has also been developed as a research paradigm underlying the degree. This is highly compatible with action-reflection research used in development studies, and anchored research among theologians. The global MATUL has seven courses designed around internships with churches or non-profits. Each is the basis of learning one type of research process. The final research requires working with an organization, in such a way that the organisational leadership are involved in the design and hence own the final decisions based on the research. Peer group discussion of how such processes develop is an essential tool in facilitating student success.

Conscientização in Transformational Conversations

Emancipation from oppression through an awakening of the critical consciousness, based on the Portuguese term conscientização is perhaps the most significant of Freire's contributions. In English, we might rename this as *Naming the Realities*. He gave a voice to those who were oppressed, enabling them to identify and speak of those realities, so that educators, who serve them, can better enable them to battle their oppression. Conscientização means developing consciousness, but consciousness that is understood to have the power to transform reality (Taylor 1993: 52).

There are limitations to these ideas, which we use in Transformational Conversations. However we are able to go deeper than critical pedagogy, because of an understanding of spirituality. Awakening collective consciousness through social analysis is a theoretical

component. But we go deeper than Freire into wider dimensions of healing - individual, communal and cultural, and the spirituality of suffering.

The spiritual formation within *Transformational Conversations* requires educators who can go deep into facilitating (1) examination of the pain and trauma, (2) self –perceptions and (3) responses (4) of those oppressed. This parallels the concept of conscientização but is not overtly political (though sometimes it is). Should it be? Are the faculty trained in identifying the traumas of oppression and spiritual formation processes that engage these?

When achieved, critical consciousness encourages individuals to effect change in their world through social critique and political action. In addition, in the MATUL, all find liberation through the expression of Christ the healer and reconciler in the cultural domain, the political domain, the social domain, the personal domain. He is all in all.

Thus, in the MATUL, socio-economic-political analysis identifies the cause of trauma. Theological reflection identifies the nature of Christ in response – be that proclamation of repentance, prayer, community development, community organization, creation of businesses, social movements, political activism. Each can be an expression of the Christ who infuses all structures, all in all.

The social analysis then leads in two directions - to personal spiritual formation that builds from the healing of the trauma through the work of the Holy Spirit and the healing of the cross. And the expression of theology in action structures - institutional or anti-institutional outworking that theology. In the political activist field these may be developed through Community Organization. However the greater impact of the church is often in the creation not of antithetical structures but of synthetical structures within the mainstream of society, yet engaging the oppressed in the reformation of that society.

Thus, we engage in a dialectical approach, that on the one hand, like many of the prophets and Jesus, calls students into prophetic opposition to oppression, but on the other, like Daniel, David, Solomon, Nehemiah calls others to engagement within the power structure of oppressive systems. This moderates some of the extremes of Fanon and other angry activists, is based on a healthy scepticism of Marxism and the lack of its exegetical validity and practical failures of liberation theology, but learns from them, moderated through Freire's common sense approaches.

Action-Reflection Resulting in Praxis.

This action is not merely the doing of something, which Freire describes as activism. It is not simply action based on reflection. It is action which embodies qualities which include a commitment to human well being, a search for truth, and a respect for others. As such it is ethical action, requiring a theological foundation. This enables society to act in ways which produce justice and allow mankind to flourish (Taylor, 1993).

The next chapter applies these trends in educational philosophy to theology and develops the primary theological methodology underlying the MATUL. As one aspect of it we will examine the concept of doing theology through structural theology, bringing theology into institutional design and manifestations.

Scholar's Heaven, MITS, Chennai, India. Obtaining a library of 400 urban ministry books has been a goal for each school

The MATUL multiplies liberation through the expression of Christ the healer and reconciler in the cultural domain, the political domain, the social domain, the personal domain. He is all in all.

05 Transformational Conversations: Andragogy with the Urban Poor

Revolutions in human thinking are not created by new information but by new paradigms that allow more information to be fitted more fully and adequately. And revolutions in scientific paradigms can be awesome moments of cognitive dissonance.

- Harvey Conn[10]

I was sitting with an Ibanag friend reviewing the gospel that he had believed the week before. But he wasn't interested in salvation from sin. "Do you know anything about demons?" he asked. "There is one in this room. he keeps disturbing me whenever I read the scriptures." We prayed. The Spirit rushed out of the room with a great wind and out of the house.

Teaching a new believer! That is *andragogy* or adult education. It starts with the context and the people's questions about theology and how God views their context.

Theological development like the above is not lacking among the poor, but it does not look the Catholic logic of Aquinas or like German theology which was based on it. It is done largely through storytelling, proverbs, and apprenticeships.

Urban workers do theology (hermeneutics), differently to those trained in seminaries. So in getting the seminary into the slums, we would expect a new kind of andragogy -the andragogy of

the poor (which I am calling *Poorology* - tongue in cheek!!), and a new kind of theological method or new hermeneutic, underlying it that I have categorized as *Transformational Conversations*.

.

Theology begins in the truth of story — God's story, my story, our story. Over the last twenty-seven years, my involvement, first in leadership of the global AD2000 cities network mentoring city leadership teams then the Encarnação network of urban poor mission leaders has prompted the evolution of a new hermeneutic – new at least for Evangelicals. This chapter develops the concept of a *transformational conversation hermeneutic*. This is then applied to the genesis of the MATUL program globally.

I discovered urban Christian workers constantly struggling with the sense of "irrelevance" of their training in systematic theology and its dissonance from the nature of the God of action they followed. In contrast they loved building collective theologies from their stories. I build the theory from such tensions by defining my terms and relating these tensions to four polarities in our perception of the godhead: his structuring and creativity, his relationship to the present and to history, his existing and acting and his transcendence and immanence.

Transformational Conversations

The phrase "transformational conversations" was sparked by Brueggeman's comments about intertextuality as "an ongoing conversation that is as urgent and contemporary as the present moment, but it is also a conversation that stretches over the generations" (1997:78-79). This study regards theology as both diachronic "conversations" (over the generations) and synchronic conversations (one time, across cultures). It defines urban theology as communal conversations with the potential for social transformation.

The three circles in the image on the next page link three conversations in a total process which I am calling a "transformational conversation": firstly, the conversation within the faith communities, secondly, the community conversation within the city and thirdly, the transformational conversation between these two.

The transformational conversation hermeneutic is fed by the metaphors and symbols, imagery and grammar, dialect and cadence of both the city and the faith community. The hermeneutic results in *defining public space* for open conversations about complex issues (I will use the term "conversation spaces"), in contrast to some approaches that reduce the scriptures to singular meanings or to absolutist slogans.

The Personality of God in Theological Style

Theology may be considered as human reflections on the nature of God. In grappling with story-telling theological processes in urban poor pastors' and city leaders' consultations we stumbled onto an understanding of doing theology as conversation. Doing theology this way consistently resolved four polarities about our perception of God better than the systematic rationalist approaches common among Evangelicals:

- Is God a rationalist philosopher or creative storyteller?
- Is God or was God? Do we know God primarily in his present actions around the globe or by ancient historical actions?
- Is God or does God?
- Is God incarnate or cosmic?

From many of the last 30 years in and out of slum areas in cities around the world I have concluded that Jesus'

Four Polarities in Theology

Is God a rationalist philosopher or creative storyteller?

Is God or was God?

Is God or Does God?

Is God incarnate or cosmic?

storytelling style embodied the primary style of teaching used among the poor. We think story, communicate story to story.

Storytelling Consultation Process

In 1996, we held a typical storytelling consultation in Mumbai with 80 leaders of urban poor ministries. Each day we would introduce the day's theme. Each worker then had ten minutes to tell his or her story. At the end of each day, we would integrate the theology and strategies that had been shared. Many worked for Western funded missions to the poor. On the side, they did what they knew really worked. It was these Indian stories of how Indians were finding solutions in their context that were crucial. At the end of the week, the whole group knew we had developed a genuine Indian theology and praxis of working with the poor.

In integrating urban poor theologies, we extended this methodology of developing grassroots theology, simply labelled as "storytelling theologies."

This requires a theological facilitator trained in ethno-theological perspectives and able to work with leadership in designing insider-outsider reflection processes. The role of the trained theologian is thus not that of the expert coming with truth, but as:

The reflector and thematizer, the one who is able to provide the biblical and traditional background that will enable the people to develop their own theology (Bevans, 1996:51).

I would add that the theologian must come as revivalist, bringing the presence of God, for such theologies have been developed much on our knees. These gatherings are often filled with a sense of the presence of God, so that the theology evolved is not simply cognitive and communal but experiential, healing, creating unity and love. At a leadership level, the process becomes more refined, systematic and rationalised.

From Stories To Global Theology

From 1991-1996, as part of the AD2000 city network, a global team of city leaders from most continents extended the "storytelling" method to city leadership consultations in other regions and cities. From these were developed urban theologies and urban strategies (Grigg, 1997b).[11] At this level, the complexity increases. We drew from stories given in multiple city contexts. I remember sitting with the leadership team for five days in 1993, identifying strands that seemed to keep twisting with other strands, becoming braids that eventually linked to major themes. The themes became paramount in the final written theology. The outcome was a globalized theology and strategy reproduced now in a number of cities.

The theologies are not developed in a vacuum. The synchronic are based on the diachronic. Participants come with previous formal or informal theological training that draws on systematic and biblical theologies, for these remain foundational. What they had never been able to express was the outworking of that theology into new indigenous theologies for their decade (thus answering the second query, "Is God or does God?" by a transition to the present and synchronic). These new theologies are not grounded in a single denominational view imported from another continent, but from indigenous expressions within the workers' own people and land. They often contradict their own views developed from imported formal training. Thus communal ownership occurs.

Such theologies develop comprehensive themes of city leadership, holistic ministry among the poor, urban poor church life, etc. This comprehensiveness is not because the theologies are developed with systematic logic, from a foundational web of belief, but because the stories cover the essential range of current issues, related to a given theme, identifying a new web of belief. Stories also gave a warm human sense of truth, honed from both Scripture and involvement. "Systematic theology.

Struggles with "storytelling theology" led me to "transformational conversations" as a more encompassing description. Stories are part of wider urban conversations.

The Labouring Poor: The Deserving Poor!!

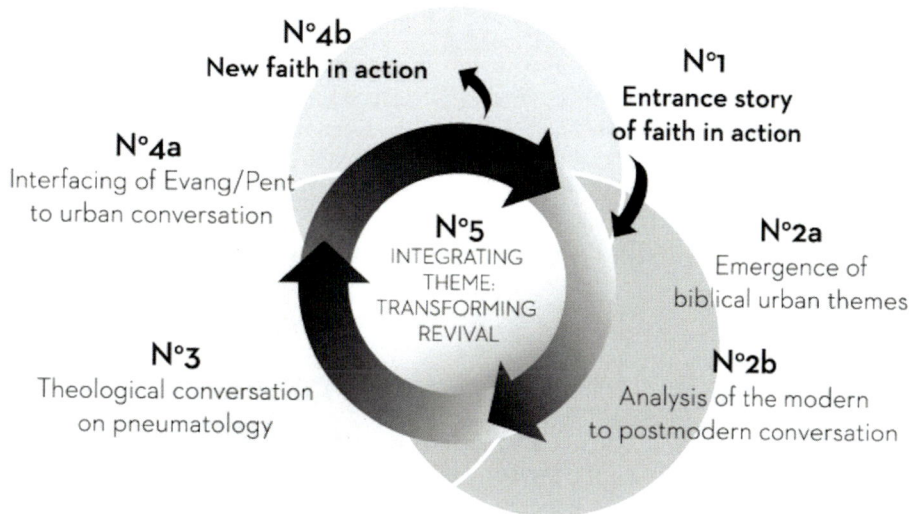

N°4b
New faith in action

N°1
Entrance story
of faith in action

N°4a
Interfacing of Evang/Pent
to urban conversation

N°5
INTEGRATING
THEME:
TRANSFORMING
REVIVAL

N°2a
Emergence of
biblical urban themes

N°3
Theological conversation
on pneumatology

N°2b
Analysis of the modern
to postmodern conversation

Above: The steps for developing a transformational conversation on the relationship of Holy Spirit and city. It begins in an action story (1). From reflection on the action, biblical urban themes develop (2a). This leads to an interface between the urban conversation (2b), the communal context and Scripture. A faith community conversation on pneumatology (3) develops from that entrance story. In turn, this leads to an interface between these two conversations on the Spirit and the city — the transformational conversation (4a). This creates a new praxis (4b).

Below: Using the concept to provide a research framework.

Transformational Conversations
Research Process

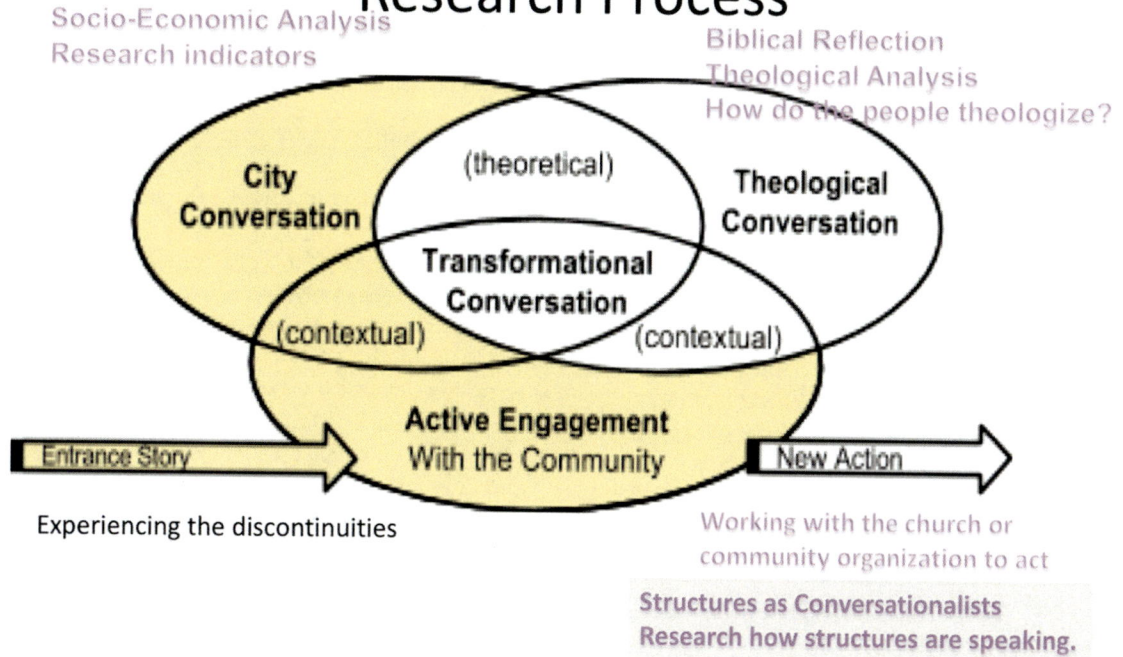

Socio-Economic Analysis
Research indicators

Biblical Reflection
Theological Analysis
How do the people theologize?

City
Conversation

(theoretical)

Theological
Conversation

Transformational
Conversation

(contextual)

(contextual)

Active Engagement
With the Community

Entrance Story

New Action

Experiencing the discontinuities

Working with the church or
community organization to act

Structures as Conversationalists
Research how structures are speaking.

Stories, Chaos and Multivariate Urban Contexts

This illustrated a major shift in urban theology from the stability and continuity of rural theologies (emphasis on God is, the God of being and stability) that have been the context of the historic church, to the ongoing discontinuities and chaos of the megacity (emphasis on God does, the God of action and change). Ariovaldo Ramos, Brazilian Evangelical leader, commented once to me, "since the city is always somewhat chaotic, an urban theological response should also be somewhat chaotic."

My father, a scientist, left a book around on chaos theory in mathematics. Chaos theory developed because of the nature of multivariate analysis — small perturbations in starting conditions lead to extensive divergences in ending conditions, apparently random, but actually following clear mathematical rules, such as in predicting weather conditions across the earth (Gleick, 1987). Cities are multivariate. Indeed, urban planning contains a whole science of fractal geometry based on multivariate analysis, that when applied to the apparently chaotic emergence of city forms enables planning predictions (Batty & Longley, 1994). The parallel concept is multivariate theologies.

In Brazil during this study, I discovered that some Latin theological methodology has also progressed from the intrusion of Marxist analysis into Catholic theology through liberation theology. Fr. João Batista Libanio in a Brazilian Catholic theology of the city, *As Lógicas da Cidade* (The Philosophic Structures of the City (2001)), affirms the approach of beginning from stories. He expands on Foucault's idea (1972:10) about seeking discontinuities beneath grand themes and relating them back to the continuity of historic theologies:

> *We opt for a reading (of theology, of the city) that creates discontinuity before we create order. This is in contrast to two very different ideological options of our time… One traditional reading prefers order, continuity… The other posture, with a modern tinge, specializes in the unity of thought of neoliberalism. This also announces changes but at their heart, these changes only maintain continuity. It fixes on a unified structural model of the city. (2001: 23 tr. from Portuguese mine).*

This concept of multiple discontinuities, multiple variables, causing us to stop in our tracks because they are different or perplexing, distinguishes urban theology.

The figure on the previous page expands the steps for developing a transformational conversation on the relationship of Holy Spirit and city. It begins in an action story (1). From reflection on the action, biblical urban themes develop (2a). This leads to an interface between the urban conversation (2b), the communal context and Scripture. A faith community conversation on pneumatology (3), develops from that entrance story. In turn, this leads to an interface between these two conversations on the Spirit and the city — the transformational conversation (4a). This creates a new praxis (4b).

Multiple Story Conversations

However, if multivariate analysis in chaos theory produces beautiful art out of apparent discontinuities, can an over-arching pattern be seen in the Scriptures? This highlights a historic hermeneutic problem of the search for a unifying centre. Osborne states,

> *As the interlocking principles between strata of the biblical period become visible, the patterns coalesce around certain ideas that bridge the gaps between the individual witnesses. However, it is very uncertain whether any single theme or concept stands at the apex of biblical theology. Many believe that the complete lack of consensus demonstrates that a cluster of ideas, rather than a single theme, unites all others (1991: 282).*

If there is no single theme, can multivariate theologies be patterned? William Temple utilised a concept of drama:

What we must completely get away from is the notion that the world as it now exists is a rational whole: we must think of its unity not by the analogy of a picture, of which all the parts exist at once, but by the analogy of a drama where, if it is good enough the full meaning of the first scene only becomes apparent with the final curtain: and we are in the middle of this.[12].

Another perspective was to examine stories within multiple contextual theologies in both Scriptures and everyday contexts. This theological storytelling or conversational approach led us to a more fruitful practical approach, since most Evangelical/Pentecostal preaching is populist, from contextual story to biblical story, rather than systematic.

The pattern of transformational theology thus be-

Fractal Cities: Echoes of the God - Conversation in systematic multivariate integrations that predict urban futures. The wave forms of the God who spoke at creation continue to produce new urban forms.

Above: Delauny Triangulation © Copyright Fractal Angel and licensed for reuse under this Creative Commons Licence.

Below: Mandallaub 3D Creative Commons CC0 Licence

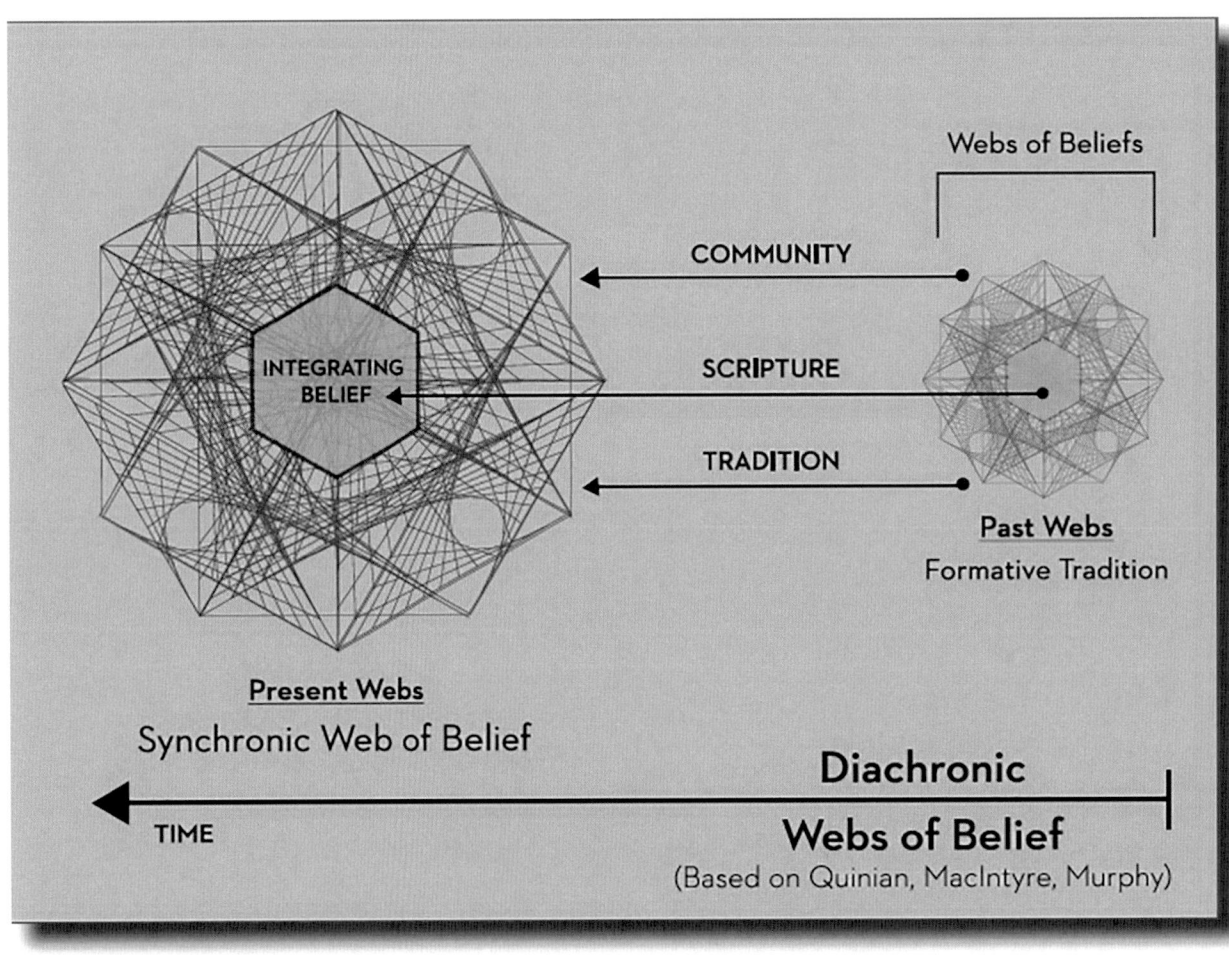

Present Webs
Synchronic Web of Belief

Diachronic
Webs of Belief
(Based on Quinian, MacIntyre, Murphy)

Web of belief analysis: In synchronic (present time, global) analysis, the integrating truth is validated by comparison of theologies across cultures. Multiple historic Christian communities and traditions feed these. In contrast, validation in traditional diachronic analysis is against past traditions derived from a formative tradition. The particular community of faith, reflecting on both Scriptures and traditions informs and validates each web of belief.

comes a dancing, multifaceted conversations, rising from the lowest classes into multiple sectors of society. It is like a series of candles that flame into life in ten thousand corners of the city. The mapping of this urban conversation cannot simply be a search for a grand theme but for multiple simultaneous interwoven themes and within them tens of thousands of vignettes.

But what should the dance, the drama, the conversation, be called? Brueggeman's concept of the unifying substance of the Old Testament as a plurality of voices led to an expanded hermeneutic for transformational conversation as the interface of that biblical plurality of story with the plurality of urban conversations.

Similarities to Narrative Theology

Narrative theologies give us some exegetical tools for step 2 in figure on the opposite page. Narrative theology in the second half of the twentieth century developed as a crossover of ideas from literary theory to become popular as an interpretative approach to the biblical stories.[13].

In the plot, coherence, movement and climax that characterize a story, narrative theology sees a way to overcome the problems theology creates for itself through its subservience to discursive reasoning (Fackre, 1983:340).

Evangelical theologians have recently been more receptive to a liberal exegetical concept of "narrative" (Van Engen, 1996:44-70). However, problems exist. Only parts (admittedly large) of the Hebrew Old Testament, the Gospels and Acts are narrative in style. Pauline and Johanine theology are both conceptual. The Wisdom literature is of a very different genre. Thus a purely narrative focus reduces the range of the God-side of a transformational conversation purely to story. The proverbs (of Solomon) and poetry (of David), the rhetorical questions (of Job), the pathos (of Jeremiah) and rationality (of Paul) must all be aspects of the conversation.

Thus, in seeking a better phrase than "storytelling" I have chosen not to use "narrative theology." It is too emotionally loaded for Evangelicals and too limited in its biblical compass.

Synchronic or Diachronic Validation

In answering the second question, "Is God or was God?" I recognise that philosophic and systematic theologies tend to be diachronic, testing for validity against historical patterns of theology back to the Scriptures. All theology must pass this test to some extent. In theology within a context of historic roots in traditional Western Europe, diachronic approaches are appropriate.

In contrast, practical, pastoral, contextual and mission theologies prefer to start with contemporary stories of the day (real stories = truth) and then find biblical truths and stories responding to these. As the global village of the 20th century shifts into the urban millennium, the verification of theology has moved from the above diachronic perspective to a synchronic perspective where we contrast theology across cultures in a single time-frame. When operating globally, those of us doing theology largely share e-mail networks enjoying collective paradigms. This process often moves too rapidly for formal publishing.

> *Recently, Biblical theologians have responded to social change by increasingly speaking about the active "God of redemption history" in contrast to categories of the "God of being" of classic theology. This raises the question about whether foundationalism (building rationally from some foundational truth) has failed[14] as the basis for theological study. In a post-modern world, history as a rational construct has been found wanting by some (see discussion in Hagner, 1998; Perdue, 1994), so ceases for many to be a valid basis for testing truth — but both rationalist liberal and evangelical theological study are deeply rooted in historical paradigms.[15] However, there are other routes to rationality than Cartesian foundationalism, which requires beliefs to rest on verifiable evidence and deductions from inarguable foundations (Vanhoozer, 1995:11).[16]*

Berger, Berger and Kellner's, *The Homeless Mind* (1973) demonstrates the development of linear rationalism as a primary cultural mode of thought within modernism. This contrasts with holistic categories of lowland Filipino thought (Lynch, c1979), representative of many peasant cultures. I have expanded these ideas in the psychology of slum-dwellers in *Cry of the Urban Poor* (Grigg, 1992/2004 ch. 15,16).

Web or Building?

A helpful model to release us from the modernist mindset of the theological fraternity is that of "knowledge as a web or net"[17] with neither foundation nor starting point (Quine & Ullian, 1978). Quine argues that non-foundational theology fits the way Christian

Urban Missions Research using Transformational Conversations

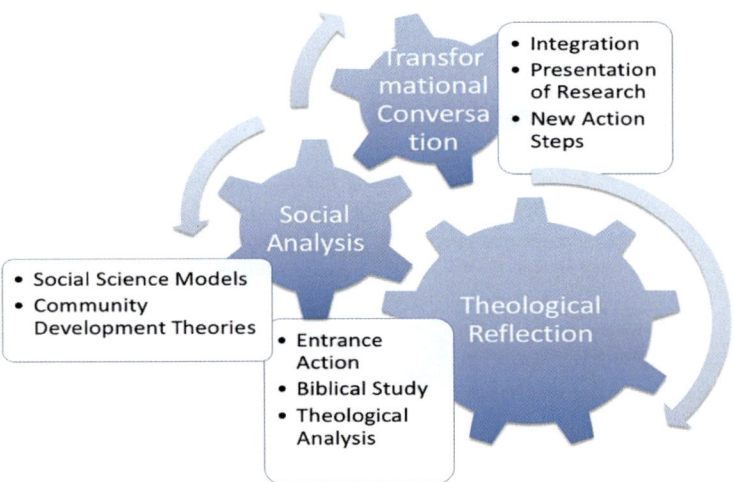

A simplified research model of Transformational Conversations

faith and practice generally operates. This requires attention to patterns inherent in beliefs and practices rather than a general theory of rationality. Since knowledge is seen as a web, there is not the question of the building collapsing if one piece of knowledge is found wanting. The stories must mesh, but need not necessarily do so in a rationalistic linear manner from a foundational point.

This web approach better describes global thought processes. Filipino or Maori cultures like most band, tribal or peasant societies are story-based, holistic in discerning truth. The aberration has been the Western nations' loss of story as primary vehicle for truth.

As Newbigin says about Western imposition of principles on biblical interpretation:

> *Our European culture (with its large non-biblical component) predisposes us to think of the biblical stories primarily as illustrative of principles which can be grasped conceptually and which enable us to remain in orbit after the supporting illustrations have been jettisoned. To live with the Bible, however, means to recognize that it is the story which is primary and irreplaceable, a story of which we and our contemporaries are a part and that the "principles" are not the enduring realities behind the story but rather the time conditioned attempts of a*

people at particular moments in the story to grasp its meaning (1981:357).

This is not a rejection of rationality. However, it is an understanding that rationality need not be linear and foundational, but can be holistic.

Nancey Murphy (1997:120) develops MacIntyre's (1988) description of tradition, to give a three dimensional, (what I call a "helical") model linking the diachronic and synchronic components. In transformational conversations, we mesh synchronic Quinian web analysis with diachronic analysis, interfacing the historic conversations with the present web. The storytelling consultations involve people trained in diachronic theologies, yet immersed in urban contexts, providing a multi- traditional background to the synchronic processes.

Incarnate or Cosmic?

This helps answer the third question, the dialectic of cosmic Christ and incarnate Son.

Urban missiologists generally insist that transcendence is rooted in incarnational living. We share a strongly held value that following Jesus demands this.

But some of us while living in the story-telling environment of the poor, also gravitate to linking the stories

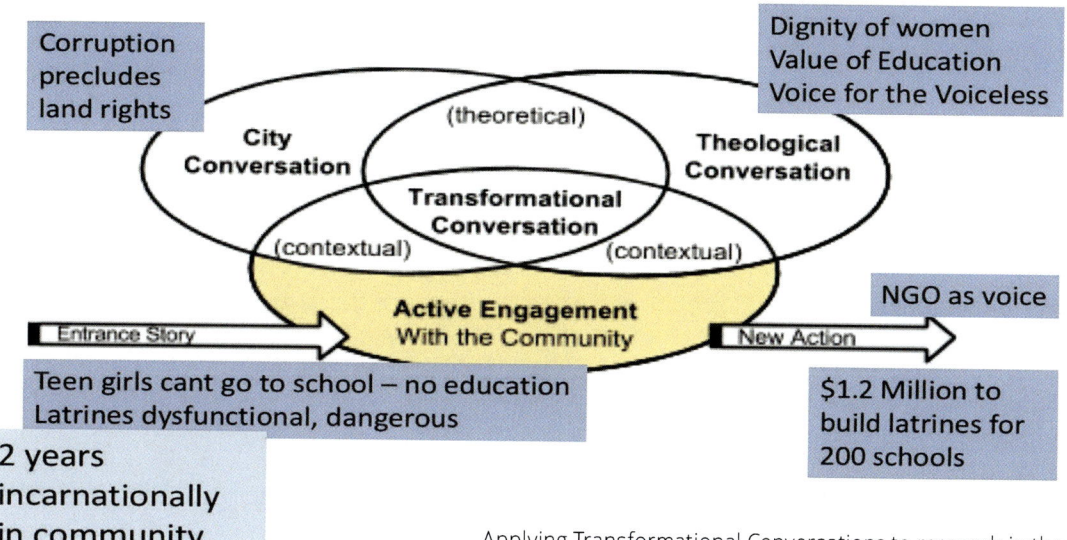

Transformational Conversational Thesis
School Latrines in Kibera Slum, Nairobi

Applying Transformational Conversations to research in the Nairobi slums, research project of Alissa Maalika

to global systematic theologies based on principles and philosophy. This reflects not just Western rationalism accentuated by rationalist modernisation but the mind of Christ who structures and organizes the universe. In his image, we intuitively search beyond the stories for supra-theological truths to connect our contextual theologies to one another.

The final stage of development of a biblical theology is the identification of an archetypal concept(s) or unifying themes behind the diverse documents.... Many believe that the complete lack of consensus demonstrates that a cluster of ideas, rather than a single theme, unites all the others (Osborne, 1991:282).

Thus in answer to the third question, "Is God cosmic or local God? Transcendent or immanent?" we recognize the necessity of both poles, but among urban workers keep the emphasis on story for we find the storytelling carries living theology better than global rationalism.

Bottom-up Contextual Theologies

This leads to the next concept. Transformational Conversations exist within a genre of contextual theology. Urban missions theology is, by its very label, contextual theology. In reality, all theologies are in essence contextual:

The Bible is a library of books and consequently of theologies. The Hebrew Scriptures are made up of Yahwist theology, Elohist theology, Priestly theology, Deuteronomic theology and Wisdom theologies, prophetic theology, exilic theology... the New Testament includes Pauline theology, Johanine theology — to name but a few (Bevans, 1996: 3).

Systematic theology itself is a contextual theological genre, with its Western, Aristotelian roots, philosophic context, establishment environment and so on.

Is God or Does God? Conversations as Action Theologies

The fourth question in establishing this hermeneutic theory is, "Is God or does God?" This is at the heart of praxis theologies. City transformational conversations begin in missional action where we seek to respond in godly manner to a need or an issue in the city. That is biblical. Theology, the knowledge of God, flows from obedience. This is part of the unspoken hermeneutic of Pentecostal theology, part of the "but does it work?" syndrome.

Like the incarnate Word, we live out conversations. Moreover, the incarnation is communal, hence structural. Structures are indicators of the realities of our theology, an anchoring into earthiness, demonstrating the God-humanity-creation linkages of a full-orbed theology.

Lawyers In Christ

51

As an example of discerning or creating a transformational theology, we could take the legal sector of New Zealand. I first asked several Christian lawyers for stories of how the Holy Spirit has led them into the public arena as Christians in an anti-Christian environment. Doing this collectively helped identify the first themes of a transformational conversation in the legal sector — themes that in their professional isolation they have been unable to identify. For lawyers work alone much of the time.

However, from the entrance stories we must press on through the conversational process to new action stories, for God is a God of action. That means enabling the lawyers to engage fully in conversation between the Scriptures and the legal sector of the city. Part of that conversation is conversation as structure. Two evangelical Christian law firms have become the core of that structure and worked with Australian counterparts to put together consultations of Christian lawyers every second year, focused on the details of Christians in the legal environment.[18]

Theology as Urban Structures

This study explores the idea that major urban conversations are conversations of ideas embodied in structures. Sustaining and expanding the structural base numerically and in quality is essential for ongoing social influence. The perception of entrepreneurial success, momentum and structural expansion is part of gaining credibility in the post-modern cultural milieux. Those who lead larger structures often gain necessary credibility to speak to higher levels of city leadership. More than image, the reality of numbers of people on the ground, with capacity to speak, expands the potential of meaningful conversation at critical social junctures.

This study proposes that should that be the case, conversation may ensue — if the theological hermeneutics enable the conversationalists to impart significant meaning in their conversation. A discussion with a battered mother about the dignity of personhood from Genesis 1 and Psalm 139 while watching our kids score goals at Saturday soccer is only possible if I understand the theology of the meaning of personhood. The same principle is true at a structural level in the city.

Implications for the MATUL

Transformational Conversation Hermeneutics, a paradigm for creating new post-modern theologies, is rooted in the nature of God. Bringing together the stories, then identifying and reflecting on themes enables conversations within the community of faith, within the post-modern urban context and between the two.

The MATUL was originally conceptualized as a bottom-up story-telling theological degree based on these principles. Following the scenarios above, most courses are expected to be 1/3 Biblical story/theology, 1/3 practice, and 1/3 technical reflection. In practice this is feasible in the more theoretical subjects such as *Urban Realities*, but involves less theology in the practicum. The first course on **Biblical Theology in Urban Contexts** lays an initial framework, working right through the scriptures from a story-telling perspective, and utilizing the locus of theology as primary being from among the poor and oppressed. It trains the students in entering the community seeking the stories of the people, and seeking to relate the Biblical stories to these.

Drift in the Design
To define a theological degree utilizing stories as the basis of theology is a serious threat to the presuppositions of the theological fraternity (to whom I have paid my dues). The immediate response is to ask, "where is Theology 1,2,3, Church History 1,2,3 Old Testament 1,2,3, New Testament 1,2,3?" The conclusion is commonly, "Perhaps we could put your emphasis as a course in Urban Missions in the electives section?"

Secondly, exegetical methods is based entirely on modernist rationalism. So to build theology form action appears to be illegitimate. To build it around story doubly illegitimate.

To avoid these issues, we have defined the degree as in MA in *Urban Leadership*. Theologians are happy to work with a bastard child, as that does not challenge their legitimacy as sons of Augustine. They like my paper contrasting Jesus-style theologizing with a Platonic approach, and while they cannot implement that approach easily within the discipline, are most excited to do so outside the boundaries.

Faculty Training in Transformational Conversation Approaches.

The immediate difficulty is that theologians at our MATUL partner schools have not always been trained in a teaching style based on conversation and story. They are used to didactics based on systematics. There has often been little development in spiritual or character formation processes and evaluation.

A second dilemma is that faculty at partner schools, who are specialists in the practical specialization are poorly formed in theological process, and application of missiological principles to their disciplines. Thus course syllabi development from practitioner-experts has also often reproduced expertise in the practitioner's field, but with only an occasional nod to the scriptures. "We are an academic program and the spiritual/theological is assigned to the chapel services". One dean advised, "we need to eliminate course objectives related to spiritual formation". Another advised that this missions program was "too missional". Another that we were "too committed to pastoral care".

The primary solutions to this latter have been to:
• Seek to train directors of partner schools in mentoring faculty in course writing that includes 1/3 theology based on a Transformational Conversations approach.
• Seek to partner theologians and practitioners to team teach in each course.

Given this theological methodology, our next question is how do we then frame the domain of urban poor missiology? How is this different to urban missions? Or community development? Or church growth? How do these domains feed into it? How far are we in its definition?

A simple dream: A city in prosperity and peace. But seeing the prosperity and peace, the latest global empire decided to buy up the land and dispossess the poor. The struggle is never-ending. Adobestock

06

Creating an Academic Domain of Urban Poor Missiology

- Developing criteria for establishing a new domain.

- Describing six artefacts that evidence paradigm breakthroughs that are significant in its development.

- Differentiating the domain from parallel domains.

- Documentation of the extent of research, publication, dissemination, and institutional development.

Ozgur Camgas, Train passing through Hanoi slums, Vietnam, Licensed Adobe Stock

 Defining the Domain

Mazeways

A cluster of us, after four decades of theological reflection, publication and lifestyles as prophetic activists at the coal-faces of oppression, violence and poverty among 1.4 billion slum-dwellers and 2 billion urban poor, find ourselves as inadequate but global voice in the definition of the disciplines of urban poor missiology at the beginning of an urban millennium.

This chapter is a series of reflections on these decades of catalysing a domain of knowledge that interfaces fields of faith and fields of action in the slums. The catalyst for this reflection was personal - a request to demonstrate faith integration at a professorial level through a portfolio of artefacts, so forgive me if this chapter, like the first, is personal reflections.

The reflections will cover:.
• developing criteria for establishing a new domain.
• describing six artefacts that evidence paradigm breakthroughs that are significant in its development.
• differentiating the domain from parallel domains.
• documentation of the extent of research, publication, dissemination, and institutional development.

I am using *domain* to indicate a loosely bounded set of actions, thoughts, influences, champions, academic *fields*. It is more than a single field. These terms are used loosely in the literature.

Criteria in Establishing a New Domain

In trying to understand my three creative children, I picked up **Creating Minds** (1993) by Howard Gardner, of multiple intelligences fame, in which he analyses Freud, Einstein, Picasso, Stravinsky, Eliot, Graham and Gandhi as genii, each in some ways creating domains of knowledge. His search was to explore creativity, but some of his conclusions help to frame the progressions in development of cultural domains of knowledge.

The following is my summary of his research: An exemplary creator has (1) an earlier period of a creative breakthrough that creates a new paradigm, and (2) a later breakthrough into a broader paradigm, then (3) decadal paradigmatic contributions. These begin (3) in the camaraderie of activism, of organizing, of stimulating others to new heights, then crystallize into (4) retreat into a realm of special interest. At this point the creative becomes isolated, sensing he/she is on the verge of breakthrough, working isolated from peers, yet craves cognitive and affective support, so that he/she can retain her bearings. (5) Often there is a breakdown. (6)"There

may be an amalgam of creativity and hard-headedness", (i.e. generally they are a pain in the butt) and there is (7) a concern for self-promotion of their work for good or for narcissistic reasons. (8) If, after the second breakthrough, the domain is wide open, the creator retains the opportunity to continue to create. (9) He indicates ten years between the paradigms.

These relate to Gardner's focus on the creative individual. But we have developed this domain as a cluster of leaders linked globally. I am also suggesting other criteria for creating a domain of activist knowledge, or faith in action:

Filling a Need: There is a hole in our (written, culturally transmittable) knowledge - with insignificantly integrated knowledge in that hole. There is a felt need for such a domain of knowledge among leaders actively engaged in that arena. That hole causes some degree of academic dissonance. Gardner indicates the realm of dissonance is an essential source of creativity.

Definition: The domain can be defined in contrast with concomitant fields.
• Significant definition has occurred within multiple disciplines or fields developed within the domain, and these can also be identified within or against other concomitant domains.
• Breadth: It includes a manageable breadth of topics including new fields of knowledge or disciplines.
Sustainable institutional support has been developed: for broad dissemination as evidenced in:.
• organisational support for operational implementation.
• Coalition and standards for profession or academic accreditation
• Opposition from established leaders of concomitant paradigms or domains.
Knowledge has been integrated, published, disseminated. As evidenced in:.
• Integration: New paradigms and fields developed
• Publication: # and depth of publications, and their impact
Dissemination:.
• # of training modules and # of locations globally, # of trainers
• multiplication of the knowledge by # of publications of another generation
• institutional structuring of the disciplines and the domain.
Modelling in global and national conversations
• A structured central global cadre fostering continued development.

The following discussion shows need, definition, institutional support, integration, publication, dissemination, differentiation, modelling and formation of a cadre. At the same time, there is also a profound sense of inadequate

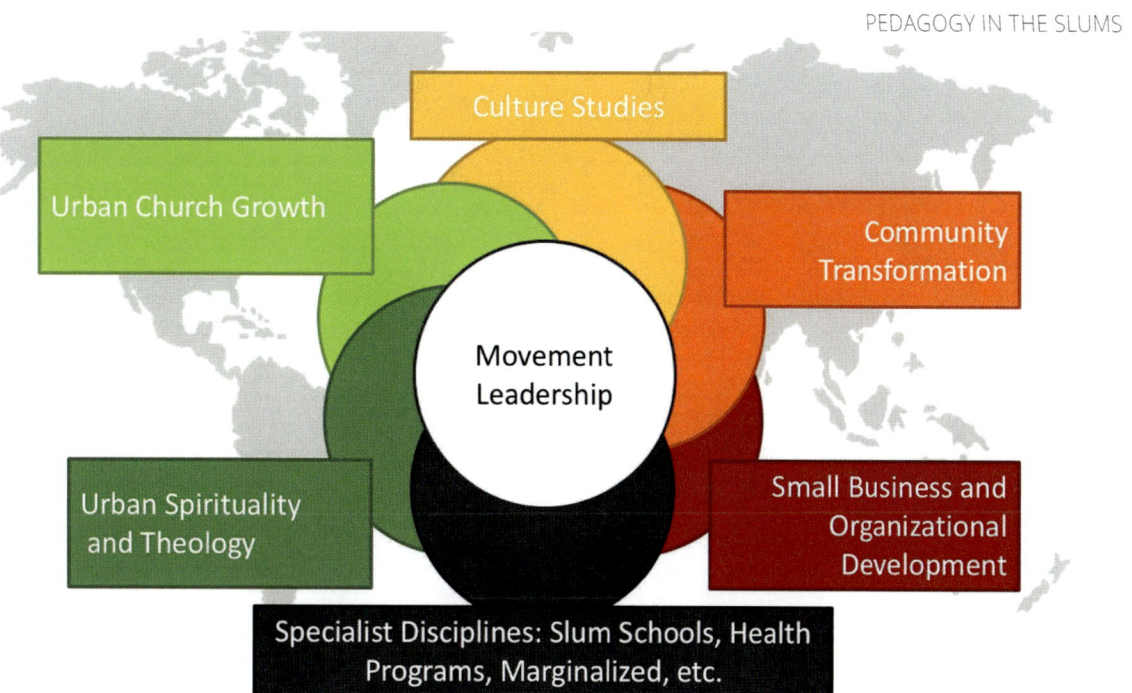

Fields within the domain of Urban Poor Missiology and the MATUL

production, institutional fragility and lack of empowerment, compared with the immensity of the task.

To demonstrate these, I will focus on six artefacts within my own works, that have involved the creation of new paradigms, as illustrative (and hopefully wihthout too high an opinion) of quality, a depth of concept and breadth of action derived from those concepts. Comments and references to sources on each of these are expanded beyond this paper on the website of artefacts at www.urbanleaders.org/Portfolio.

Structuring the Domain

The initial aim was to come up with generic training materials that could multiply rapidly. Each grassroots consultation of 25-100 pastors and workers usually resulted in a doubling of the number of churches - 1198 new churches over three years at one count. This lead to another progression in the development of the domain: intuitively I understood that the Masters level is a place to integrate the breadth of a domain. We needed to get the seminary into the slums, but the style of seminary education would be dramatically different to the traditions handed down from Catholicism through the Bible School movement.

It began in 2002 with a gathering in Brazil, of 25 leaders of works, and another in Bangkok in 2004 with 48 global leaders of these and other partners. It involved the instigation in 2006-7 in Manila, Nairobi and Chennai, India,

of the MA in Transformational Urban Leadership. It has expanded currently (at MA or BA levels) to eight universities or seminaries globally (Five of which are functioning), and multiple grassroots training processes linked to these. This has provided a context to create the domain of urban poor missiology as a separate domain from urban missiology.

Definition and Breadth

Within that domain, I identified 23 fields, which are in themselves new sub-fields of urban poor theology and praxis. These I had derived from analysing responses at 22 urban poor consultations in the late 1990's in 20 global cities. I would ask participants what training they had, what they desired, what they needed. After deleting the desire to have all that Bible schools offered (which generally reflected imported Western structures), 23 fields were evident.
.

These fields, overall, mostly dwelt within urban missiology, so delineating the domain itself as an entity in its own right has some difficulties. In developing the MATUL, we reduced these to 15 courses. These get reduced further in each school as traditional theologians, generally without understanding that Germanic systematice theology is a subfield of contextual theology, demand the addition of systematic theology and biblical studies courses. The tension between the new wine skin and the old nearly split one faculty over 15 years. Reflections on these issues resulted in the unpublished though widely disseminated articles, *Jesus Seminary in the Slums* (2003) and *Radical Restructuring of the Seminary* (2004).

Go to www.matul.org for an overview of the course development ; to www.urbanleaders.org/ma for the content of the commission gatherings and to www.urbanleaders.org/Portfolio/PortfolioMATUL.html for further analysis of processes.

Sustainable Infrastructure

These fields (and a field of reconciliation that was added, but not yet implemented), and 15 courses, became the basis of a website of scores of presentations by the directors and some of the 40 faculty delivering courses at partner schools within the coalition at our annual MATUL COmmission gathering. Each school functions within its own operational and financial system (there are no dependencies) and under the accreditation system of its own country.

Breadth of Dissemination

In 2015, the directors of the MATUL programs meeting in the yearly MATUL Commission determined to concentrate their graduates on grassroots development, so currently we are exploring how to expand dissemination of the master's level content out to 10,000 in the slums at a grassroots level of delivery.

Differentiating the Domain

Urban Missiology expands the evangelical mindset into handling heterogeneity within the urban environment and involves a holistic integration of evangelism with response to structural evils (Conn, 1993: 96-104). This wider field of Missiology itself covers the theology of mission, history of missions, social sciences particularly anthropology, development studies and church growth. As such, by definition it is a faith-integrated domain.

However, the term, faith integration, used in the *Christian Community Colleges and Universities* (CCCU) circles in the US, is a strangely unknown phrase in urban mission's circles, where the term "holistic mission" would perhaps be more used to cover similar ideas.

Similarly, in urban missions circles we do not utilize the word "faith" as primarily a noun to define a belief system but as an element of a verbal phrase, we speak of our "faith in action" and would affirm Gregory Leffel's phrase, "Faith Seeking Action" or, "Faith-based organization" or, Alexia Salvatierra's "Faith-rooted Organizing" (2014) which has an emphasis on active engagement that is based on the rationality of belief

systems.

Differentiation of Research Methodology

As the crowning process of a master's' degree, perhaps the heart of faith integration is most deeply manifest in our research paradigms. It is no mean feat to create a paradigm that succeeds to a level of a balanced integration of both theological reflection and social theory.

Urban missions research has post-modern allies in sociology and in various disciplines, including theology, in utilizing "grounded theory". Some of us also are deeply influenced by the complexity of Freire and his pedagogical descendants in Critical Discourse, Critical Pedagogy, Critical Race Theory – the "critical" referring less to logicisms and more to seeking solutions to radical discontinuities within the culture, the earthquake lines of pain that mark the struggles of urbanization.

The previoius chapter, that developed the complexities of Transformational Conversations is extended by other unpublished works which convert these into a research methodology. These are the ten-year culmination academic breakthrough of the story-telling paradigm shift.

But the field of research paradigms is so crowded one would be unwise to claim it as a unique paradigm. There are parallel approaches in the "Pastoral Cycle" used among Anglicans in Africa (Heriot, 1974). Van Engen's (1996) crossover to evangelicalism of a liberation theology approach derived from Freire, was published at a similar time to my development of this paradigm.

I would humbly suggest that perhaps Transformational Conversations appears to better capture the essential nature of the urban theological process by including incarnational models, discontinuity, story, communal exegesis across the theological spectrum in a city, action-based outcomes, the institutional outworking of the emergent theology and affirmation of grassroots orality as a valid form of theological reflection.

In analysing Transformational Conversations as a postmodern theological process creating webs of belief (based on Quine's concept of knowledge as a web or net with neither foundation nor starting point (1978)), I have described it using an asynchronic framework. It is not dissimilar to the Wesleyan quadrilateral favoured by Azusa Pacific Seminary – though Wesley had never heard of it (Grigg, 2009, pg 29)!.

See www.urbanleaders.org/Portfolio/PortfolioConversations.html artefact #4 for further analysis.

Relationship to the Domains of Community Development and of Global Development Industry

I am a community development practitioner, every week involves me in funding or managing or surpervising or training folks in community development (now often called community transformation). As I write this I am preparing for a Micah Network gathering which brings leaders of global community development networks together.

But we face a dilemma, one I have faced over the decades. Every time we include a Community Development expert into the MATUL leadership we are faced with this dilemma. For them the MATUL is a Community Development degree. That is all they see! Holistic mission is reduced in their minds to the transfer of wealth from rich to poor and the resourcing of projects. The issue is poverty!

A parallel and perhaps greater challenge is the theroetical relationship of the *Urban Poor Missiology* domain to the *Global Development* domain. This is a big domain, with big moneys, lots of papers and research and academics. Foucault's "knowledge is power" can be reversed, "power is knowledge, defines knowledge, defines agendas.".

Urban poor missiology clearly draws from development agendas in areas of biblical responses to AID's, Land Rights, Advocacy etc. Yet again there is a necessary fight for distinctiveness. The global development agenda as defined by the UN, integrates the global NGO's including Christian NGO's, yet my students debate whether the agendas are truly parallel to the Kingdom of God, as there is a global awareness that this is an industry that does not perceive the slum needs accurately and involves some very big elements of corruption. Aposltic leaders do not percive poverty as THE issue. THE issue is establishing the Kingdom of God. Cofnronting poverty is a art of that wider dimension.

My fellow slum-dwelling church-planters are *persona non-grata* in such a world. They are considered divisive; their works quaint; with little sense about the power of money, and the role of foreigners in its delivery; their gospel is of little relevance to the global development agendas. (I do not have literature to support this claim, I doubt there is any, but these statements reflect multiple conversations in the field).

The Biblical idea of the church as centre of good news and transformation is often foreign to them, as the objective is not the Kingdom of God but delivery of services or changing economic relationships (both worthy goals). The idea of evangelistic, discipling, church growth and revival movements has little to do with transferring services, so is considered irrelevant. One attempt by one dean to reduce the degree to community development was to cut the church-planting and movement leadership courses as evangelism and church growth have no bearing on NGO's.

The core structures of urban poor missiology are also at variiance with those of this industry. The idea of a spirituality based on committed communities whose priority is caring for the incarnational workers is in opposition to the idea of the development agency as a business, with NGO's as profitable non-profits run on a business model - a necessary model as their task is the delivery of resources.

The core of the urban spirituality course demonstrates another tension. Without coming from a basis of living by faith, community development workers are in the job market of getting contracts with NGO's - a very fragile way to live usually with year to year contracts. The idea cherished by the urban poor church-planters that through prayer, God answers and provides for his people as more long-term solid basis for engaging the poor, is outside of the development rhetoric and spirituality, despite the evidence that it is church movements pioneered by men and women who live by faith that are changing the scenario among the poor and the NGO knowledge that these religious movements are the de facto centres of delivery of programs as they have the leadership development and the training in integrity. Each time the global organizations enter a city they buy up the local pastors with foreign money to implement delivery of their programs.

The input from development workers is critical as adjuncts to give balance in the MATUL Program. Deans need to recognize that the program leadership (deans, directors, core faculty), however, needs to be delivered by those with apostolic pioneering church growth and ministry experience. The difficulty is that those in the development agencies have had the money and time to get the advanced degrees, so tend to be more available.

Contrast with Social Work

Similarly, some have immediately decided that since this is for the poor, it must be a social work degree. Those who have been trained in social work see themselves as the elite, skilled in caring for the poor - and rightly so. There is certainly a discipline and market for such a degree, so if a school is defined by recruitment numbers to survive financially this is a good option.

The aim of social work is to deliver government services or distribute wealth through an NGO to relieve the needs of the poor. In contrast, the aim of the MATUL is to train movement leaders in multiplying holistic churches that engage the needs for the poor from within.

A part of that is common to both domains, to train leaders to deliver services. This is covered in the course on *Working with the Marginalized*. There is some crossover in the *Advocacy* course. The style of the *Final Research Project* is very similar in both degrees. Use of various social sciences in the analysis of poverty is common to both domains.

But the aim of distributing money and goods and services to individuals in need is not the same as the aim of developing leadership among the poor. This involves seeing healthy churches formed, in which leadership is multiplied. These two are the prerequisites for ethical leaders that then are able to engage needs. The engagement is through their incarnational presence in the slum community. It may involve redistribution, but it is much wider than gold and silver.

Contrast with Urban Missions

I remember being invited out of the Kolkata slums to speak at a global Lausanne conference in 1989 in Manila, which gathered the evangelical leaders from around the world. When I arrived, I discovered I had been invited to speak in the Urban Missions track. Not being very intelligent I had wondered for some years as to what Urban Missions was. It seemed very American and British, and as I talked with folks they had lots of big words. Their goals seemed to be to generate projects based on fund-raising to deliver programs to the poor though big old inner city churches in the West.

I had been pioneering urban missions for 15 years, but did not fit. Because urban missions for those of us in the third world begins on the periphery in the newer slums where there is no church and we preach and establish churches and schools then help the new

congregation engage the needs of the community and develop people through economic discipleship into a self-sustaining faith community. There were a few colonial cities like Kolkata where there was a significant urban centre church delivering such programs and the Salvation Army doing the same, but mostly we were working with church-planters pioneering new ministries.

My conclusion was that while I could talk the lingo of these Westerners, our movements did not fit and did not need to fit within urban missions. But since as Foucault said, "Knowledge is power", these leaders had termed a phrase and we were expected to kow-tow to the superior western expertise and money. They were unaware that we did not belong, so no need to offend them. Play their games! But they kept inviting us to conferences. It cost a lot of time and money. I had quietly gone back to Kolkata. Then the Lord took me to lead the AD2000 Cities Network. After several years, again I quietly dropped out, to work with where the real fruit was happening - in learning networks of urban poor pastors.

An important element to evaluate is whether urban poor missiology can be differentiated as a domain or simply a field or set of fields within the existing domain of Urban Missiology.

US Urban Missiology developed largely around Paul Hiebert, Roger Greenway and Harvey Conn in the 1980's and 1990's. The *Urban Missions* magazine that Harvey Conn edited for ten years became a central vehichle. Programs developed at several US Seminaries. Bob Linthicum, Bob Lupton and then John Perkins became spokespersons, then Ray Bakke multiplied these ideas around the globe as a Laussanne Senior Strategist.

In the US and Britain, urban missions is perhaps a holdover of a Christendom model in older denominations. This is very different to *urban poor missiology* as developed from the third world, which is built on church-planting, largely Pentecostal, among the urban poor, migrants on the city edge.

This contrast is stark, but it is unlikely that we have the capacity financially to resist the power of the US dollar and its publication machines in determining the nature of urban missions. For example, the *International Society of Urban Mission* set up some conferences in Asia, that rapidly were peopled by Westerners, run by

Westerners and published articles by Westerners in the ISUM Journal. After years of being with indigenous leaders, it was strange place to be - a different world, a different domain. I knew the people, we were friends, colaborers. They had read my works, we were welcome. But then we went back to our slums.

Stephen Burris, who edited that Journal, subsequently developed the *International Journal of Urban Transformation.* Again, this is communication among the educated elites -the urbanologists, and missiologists for whom this document is aimed. I am a Westerner, I am a writer, I am a missiologist. I love to contribute. But everything must be subject to the question whether it assists in liberating our people.

Many other attempts over the years to mesh our urban poor networks with the global urban missions networks have also ended in a disconnect. The language and style and financial capacities of well-funded, academic, highly conceptual gatherings is not relevant. This is not connected to their world. Despite that dissonance, the missions leaders in the slums are able to connect,but that does not mean they belong.

Urban Poor Missiology is thus a safe place of belonging, a separate domain with cross-overs because we are brothers seeking to transform cities.

Sustainable Structure

As mentioned, US evangelical urban missiology developed around some key figures in Ray Bakke, Roger Greenway, Harvey Conn. Bakke Graduate School developed as a major centre. Other schools

developed urban courses and some programs, but only at Eastern and Gordon-Conwell have these survived. Fuller Theological Seminary has a few courses. This leads to a question as to whether urban poor missiology can also survive in the academic institutional environment. Cost is a factor, as students are poor and working with the poor, so foundation grants are essential. Leadership is essential to both recruit students and raise the funding needed - so programs need to be lead by those with a business head.

Sustainable Publications.
Whatever develops academically is published in that Urban Missions world. So as a discipline, we have to straddle both, publishing at both the academic level, and designing training that multiplies skills at the oral and semi-literate level. The *New Urban World Journal* published articles from a number of our partners over five years. I am an advisor to a new *International Journal of Urban Transformation*, which is consistently publishing from among our people. Thus in publishing, Urban Poor Missiology can hang on the coat tails of Urban Missiology.

Differentiation
To return to the question: Is it just a field within urban missiology? It is more than a field, as we have already identified 23 fields of knowledge that are required by urban poor movement leaders. ***Thus it is a domain, but it is an overlapping domain.*** To differentiate the domains, one has to ask the question, are these fields the same as in broader urban missiology?

On the one hand, the answer is no!! Urban poor church-planting, for example, is a field in its own right, very different to the urban church in America

or England. My two works on this (*Companion* and *Cry*) remain essentially the only works on processes of church-planting in the slums.

Establishing slum schools in the global slums is a burgeoning field in TED talks but not within Urban Missions – an indication that it is a field outside of Urban Missions as it exists. But integral to Urban Poor Missiology and the MATUL.

On the other hand, the paradigm of *Transformational Conversations*, while developed in the decade before Chuck Van Engen published on processes of doing urban missiology, is of the same genre as his work. And my course on *Urban Poor Missiology* is not significantly different to what I would teach if it was Urban Missiology. The emphases are different, but the themes the same. Community Organizing fits in either category.

On the other hand, my development of the only course in the world that integrates biblical theology and praxis of engaging in land rights for slum-dwellers, is not even on the agenda of the Urban Missiologists. Land rights theology has no meaning in the US context, where housing advocacy is a highly developed field relating to complex US legal structures.

On the other hand, well-heeled, well-educated Urban Missiology will constantly subsume Urban Poor Missiology. It will buy these workers, and woo them.

On the other hand, at the end of the day, to protect our global urban poor leaders, is it wiser not to allow them to be sucked into the affluent networks and verbology?

Since one has no third hand, one remains ambivalent!! Or was that ambidextrous.

Opposition from the Establishment

Approached another way, Gerlach and Hine (1970) indicate that movements are formed in opposition to existing structures. My conciliatory nature prefers not to embrace that! The realities push one towards it!.

Establishing the domain as an entity of itself, has to do with (i) the academic integration of the whole, (ii) the establishing of a domain name, (iii) a publications vehicle, (iv) the sustaining of movements that live out the practice (v) academic institutions sustaining training.

The first (i) we have accomplished. The last (v) we have begun with eight universities or seminaries, but have found that each change of president, dean or director derails the process, so it becomes an enormously costly exercise to shore these up. For item (iv) we have

worked to establish multiple movements of urban poor church-planting independent of the middle class. But items (ii) and (iii) are meshed with the wider urban missiology controlled by US/British perspectives. That is unlikely to change.

Publishing within the Domain

One of the marks of a movement is that one's disciples begin to publish. And one's enemies seek to discredit. And others rise up and begin to fill the space, building off one's ideas without connection - for while one can reference 25 books by disciples and colaborers, there are yet many others with similar ideas in the same space who have never heard of one's writings or are unaware that one's paradigms have filtered down to them. These each bear testimony. Another testimony is Google Scholar which records 277 citations of my various works, and I am sure Scott Bessenecker, Craig Greenfield or Ash Barker have similar readerships of their urban poor books.

Others seek to analyze. Kevin Book-Satterlee in analysing the MATUL, terms his paper, ***Out of the Cloister and into the Streets: Two Partnership Models of Integrated Praxiological Andragogy in Cross-Cultural Urban Ministry.*** Each sub-field, such as working with HIV/AIDs' victims, or dealing with land rights have their own networks and authors.

Creating the Academic Infrastructure

The application of this hermeneutical approach to creating the MATUL programs globally has involved experimentation in content development; interfacing story-telling approaches with the over-arching Aristotelian logic of the academe; faculty development to internalize new paradigms, and identifying educational techniques to implement these paradigms; identifying those conversations critical to the urban poor and their public space (Grigg 2012:2).

Formation of a Domain?

Foucault's "knowledge is power" might be true, but I would suggest it is definitely true that "creation of a domain of knowledge depends on the power of capital formation". Yet, the Lord has enabled the integration of this domain without our having position, power or pesos, so one has to attribute it to the work of the Spirit as the grand capitalist creator.

To expand that idea, the decades of development of a global discipline has been dependent on building multiple capital streams: capital of integrated ideas; capital growth of publication and dissemination; moral capital in terms of trust, respect, integrity between leaders globally; social capital in terms of building a global cadre of people influenced and multiplying these ideas in networks and institutions. All of these involve financial capital.

The question of this chapter is thus, whether the building of such capital has enabled a significant empowerment of my companions among the poor for theological solutions of the world's great urban problems; or has it simply been a pursuit of personal curiosity or a pipe dream. Or, perhaps such capitalism on behalf of the poor has been so poorly executed, such that one has thrown away the gilded opportunity?

As an example of the expanding domain, and recognizing the significant contributions of others, the portfolio I developed for APU faculty purposes,[19] demonstrated:

1. *Responding to a Need:* There is a felt need for such a domain of knowledge among leaders actively engaged in the arena.
2. *Definition:* The domain can be defined in contrast with concomitant fields. Significant definition has occurred, with multiple disciplines or fields developed within the domain, and these identified against other domains. It includes a manageable breadth of topics including new fields of knowledge or disciplines. Opposition from established leaders of the previous paradigm is apparent though muted.
3. *Institutional support* has been developed. But it is questionable if it is sustainable. It is evidenced in organisational support for operational implementation in multiple schools and in grassroots learning networks. This is fostered by a cadre of deans and faculty that work as a coalition in the MATUL Commission, seeking standards for the professional delivery. Academic accreditation is nationally determined, so varies as to the maintenance of the core of the discipline as no accreditors so far have had experience in working with the urban poor.
4. *Knowledge* has been researched, integrated, published, disseminated. This has been evidenced in over 25 books from leaders in related incarnational missions, over 80 theses by students, podcasts, websites and videos of materials.
4.1.1. *Research:* Multiple research methods have been used. Transformational Conversations, ethnography, urban anthropological research methods, along with global databases on 6600 cities and the size of their slums, and literature analysis of the growth of the slums or the emergence of postmodernism, or on a surface level, historical analysis of missiological struc-

tures, not forgetting various theological exegeses, have all fed into the above artefacts.
4.1.2. *Integration*
• 6 new paradigms are demonstrated in the next page as artifacts and there are others, such as discipling a post-postmodern culture. New fields have been developed, others have been integrated from urban missions or community development domains.
4.1.3. Personal *Publication*
• 7 books with 7 translations, two recognized as paradigm-shifting within the Missions community and two significant in the depth of theological development as it interfaces with urban issues. 34 professional articles including translation into various languages, 14 websites 121 web-based Power Points in 8 fields, 35 videos, accessed by 15,115 people. To these may be added 25 books by others, and courses by Colin Smith in Nairobi, and faculty in Manila at Asian Theological Seminary.
4.1.4. *Dissemination*
• According to Google scholar, these books and articles have been cited 246 times in academic journals (Their list excludes mission publications).
• At least 99 training modules have been taught (many multiple times) at 27 locations globally, with over 22 city network leaders and 45 faculty function as trainers.
• Multiplication of the knowledge by 15+ books by another generation, a professionally produced documentary.
• Institutional structuring of the disciplines in the MATUL in 8 schools, of which five are sustained, 3 others are enquiring.
• These are personal outputs. When we consider the breadth of the networks, these are multiplied.
5. *Movement Cadre*
• The MATUL Commission continues as a structured global cadre fostering development.

Conclusions: A Domain Formed, Multiplying, Fragile...

Expansion is dependent on the communal web of relationships and leadership to sustain them. While we have leadership networking, no leader with access to resources, incarnational experience, and academic credibility has risen to assume the global leadership integration. Periodically, the Lord lifts up one or the other, in a dispersed leadership progression. We all cheer and support as best we can.

Developing the Domain within the DMATUL

1. Grassroots Theology

2. Research

3. Social Entrepreneurship

Beloved Professor, HBI, Chennai

	COURSE TITLE	
TUL500	A Biblical Theology of Urban Mission	
TUL 584	Systematic and Contextual Theology	
TUL502	Exegetical Methods	
TUL505/506	Language and Culture Learning	
TUL520	Urban Spirituality	
TUL530	Building Faith Communities:	
TUL540	Urban Reality and Theology	
TUL550	Service with the Marginalized	
TUL555	Education'l Centre Development	
TUL560	Community Economics	
TUL620	Movement Leadership	
TUL630	Community Transformation	
TUL640	Entrepreneurial Leadership	
TUL650	Primary Health Care	
TUL655	Advocacy and Land Rights	
TUL670/5	Research Project/ Thesis	

THEOLOGICAL EMPHASIS	RESEARCH METHODS	ENTREPRENEURIAL SKILLS
Contextual & urban theological method, Biblical Theology from the perspective of the poor, oppression, disposses-sion, migration, urbanization etc.	Urban Theological Method: 1. Transformational Conversations. 2. Story-telling cultural analysis. 3. Endnote or equivalent for referencing	Engaging in community conversations
Integrating the contextual program knowledge into systematic theological constructs, Exegesis. (Determined by traditional Faculty)	Doing Theology from the Margins	Engaging in community conversations
Exegesis of one gospel (or similar Biblical studies course – determined by traditional faculty).	Exegesis underlying theological components of research	
Incarnation, multiculturalism, finding person of peace	Participant Observation: 1. Incarnational Living 2. Field Notes	Cross-cultural communication & work
Justification, sanctification, pneumatology, cross-cultural, urban, indigenous spiritualities	Cultural Analysis: 1. Mapping Community Spirituality 2. Evangelistic research	Spirituality of Entrepreneurship
Ecclesiology, Biblical leadership models, evangelism and church growth	Church Growth Analyses 1. Harvest Force and Harvest Field 2. Community analysis for evangelism. 3. Funding Plan	Collaboration, multiplication, curriculum development, delegation
Theological reflection on social science theories.	Cultural Analysis: Locating in the context of major Urban Studies theories	Community Social & Economic Research
Diaconal leadership roles in distribution and program management among the poor. Biblical reflections on widows, orphans, lame, blind, disabled.	1. Case Study Analysis 2. Organizational Analysis, 3. Participant Observational Techniques	Analysis of an NGO Structure and Leadership
Bible theology of wisdom and education as manifest in educational theories.	Gantt Chart, Participatory Observer Organizational Analysis, Interviews	Organizational Analysis of an Educational Institution
Biblical Principles of economics applied at family, community, national and international levels, impacting the poor.	Organizational Analysis	Funding research, grant writing, mobilization, Analysis of an NGO
Exegesis of Acts, Biblical leadership models, qualities, church growth.	Analysis of Principles, Literature review	Grant writing, running a conference, establishing a network, team, Publishing
Theological underpinnings of Global and Community Development sector.	Funding Plan, Project Planning	Project planning and implementation
Theology of entrepreneurship and business management.	Business Plan, Funding Plan, Financial Plan	Business Plan, Funding Plan, Financial Plan
Theology of health care.	Community Needs Analysis	Community Groups
The prophets, Biblical models of advocacy, Biblical theology of Land.	Theology of place, theology of land, biblical advocacy	Grant writing, event planning, research
Theological reflections as part of the research process, grounded theology.	Participatory urban theology: thesis proposal, writing process or project analysis community participation in research	Intrapreneurial change processes: Action-research as strategic planning tool

Artefacts in the Formation of the Domain

Artefacts can often be symbolic milestones in the definition of an academic domain. The following artefacts have been seminal to my personal exploration of the domain of Urban Poor Missiology:

Companion to the Poor (1984)

The evolution of a personal theology, translated into six languages, reprinted nearly yearly, telling the story of years entering and pioneering the first church in Manila's slums is used as a basis for defining theological and praxis paradigms for urban poor church-planting, and community transformation. This book enabled the global evangelical missions community to embrace the concept of incarnational ministry among the urban poor.

Over twenty other books (see a list in Appendix) have now been written by members of incarnational missions expanding on themes of incarnational mission. Apart from my sequel, *Cry of the Urban Poor,* none have been written on urban poor church-planting.

The Lifestyle and Values of Servants (1981)

A monograph (Grigg, 1981) that has become the foundational document for the culture and structure of several missions. It integrates the theology of apostolic motivation for incarnational mission into values and practice for Protestant incarnational missions, outworked in principles of evangelism, simplicity, justice-making.

Incarnational Urban Poor Missions(1981)

The formation of Servants to Asia's Urban Poor, Companions to the Poor, Servant Partners, Inner Change, Word Made Flesh, Kairos from Brazil, St Stephen's Society in Hong Kong, have all implemented these themes. Scott Bessenecker has sought to integrate them under the name New Friars, modelled after the preaching friars of the 13th Century.

Spirit of Christ and the Postmodern City (2009)

This book is based on a case study of four years of developing of a city leadership team of Pentecostals and Evangelicals in Auckland. It aims to map the progressions from a theology and praxis of revival to processes of transformation of a post-modern city. As such, while it is focussed on upper level leadership in cities, it created a framework for the field of urban movement leadership and the paradigm of *Transformative Revival.*

Transformational Conversations(1996)

Development of a paradigm for theological engagement with urban issues. Based on processes refined in over 30 city consultations with city leaders and urban poor workers, this is interfaced with a theory of "knowledge as webs" to generate a process that has been used by urban workers as an urban research paradigm.

Economic Discipleship(1981-2018)

A field of knowledge within urban poor missiology, of ten principles of Biblical Economics developed from 35 years teaching in the slums.

- Applied to national economic issues in New Zealand in a book, *Kiwinomics* (Grigg 2016).
- Applied to the slums in an www.*economicdisciple.org* site of podcasts for oral learners.
- Multiplied through graduate students to many churches.

The Training Commission (2002-15)

At the centre of the development of a new domain of knowledge is the formation of the Urban Poor Leaders Training Commission, a committed global cadre of program directors in 8 schools, deans and faculty practitioner-experts. They integrate and disseminate the domain. 23 fields of knowledge are evidenced in 15 courses and the processes of dissemination in MATUL Commission website discussions.

Excursis: Differentiating from Other Similar Terminology

With the explosion of knowledge, sometimes similar terms are generated in multiple fields without connection. The following is to differentiate our discussion from others using similar terms. It is not essential to the argument of the book.

Transformational Urban Leadership as a field is not a subset of business, educational or psychological leadership models.

Transformational Urban Leadership is a name determined by the initial *Encarnação Alliance Training Commission* and *Urban Leadership Foundation* in 2006 to describe **the field of urban poor missiology.** It does not pretend to include the many varieties of urban leadership or urban leadership institutions globally. It was developed through exploring the qualities of apostles, prophets, evangelists, and pastor-teachers within urban poor movement dynamics.

In contrast, James V. Downton, appears to be the first to coin the term "Transformative Leadership", a concept further developed by leadership expert James MacGregor Burns who adjusted it to "Transformational". According to Burns, transformational leadership can be seen when "leaders and followers make each other advance to a higher level of morality and motivation. Through the strength of their vision and personality, transformational leaders are able to inspire followers to change expectations, perceptions, and motivations to work towards common goals." Thus transformation implies a personal leadership style within this discipline. Bernard M. Bass (1985), extended the work of Burns (1978) by explaining the psychological mechanisms that underlie transforming and transactional leadership.

This is not incompatible with the core of our field of *Transformational Urban Leadership.* But our field is derived from church growth movements, revival movements and city leadership movement perspectives. *We envision transformation as the impact of leadership on the community, an expansion of the common good, towards the principles of the Kingdom of God. Thus it is about impact.* This may include a transformative leadership style.

Transformational Conversations in Urban Theology differentiated from those in Business, Education, Psychology.

In 1996, Viv Grigg first disseminated the concept of Transformational Conversations in *Developing an Auckland Business Theology*. One version was published in 1999 as "Transformational Conversations: Hermeneutic for Postmodern City" in the *PCBC Journal* in Australia. This was also a chapter in his PhD thesis published in 2004 and again by Emeth Press as a chapter in *The Spirit of Christ and the Postmodern City* in 2006.

Meanwhile, in 1998, Lisa Giruzzi founded her own coaching company, which later became *Transformational Conversations* (2003) offering business consulting and coaching. Her mission: causing a positive revolution in change in the workplace. Meanwhile *Integral Coaching Canada* developed the term also. This was discussed in a publication *Transformational Conversations: The Four Conversations of Integral Coaching. In the Journal of Integral Theory and Practice*, Vol 4, Issue 1, p 69-92, by Joanne Hunt.

Meanwhile in Education in 2011, Louise Taylor published an educational article for early childhood teachers, *Making Time for Transformational Conversations.* [20]

These have all been developed in parallel yet independently.

Part 3: Foci in a Movement Leadership Degree

1. *Church growth movements: pioneering holistic urban poor church-planting movements*

2. *Cross-Cultural & Urban Spirituality*

3. *Contextual grassroots theology*

4. *Creative social entrepreneurship*

5. *Community transformation*

We have explored some elements of the grassroots theology. In the next chapters we briefly identify the focus on movement leadership and explore social entrepreneurship.

Fields within the Domain

The domain contains 23 fields of knowledge. These can be identified within five main fields, and in the degree these become specific to courses. It is primarily a degree in Movement Leadership, but that has ministry and entrepreneurial and community development elements.

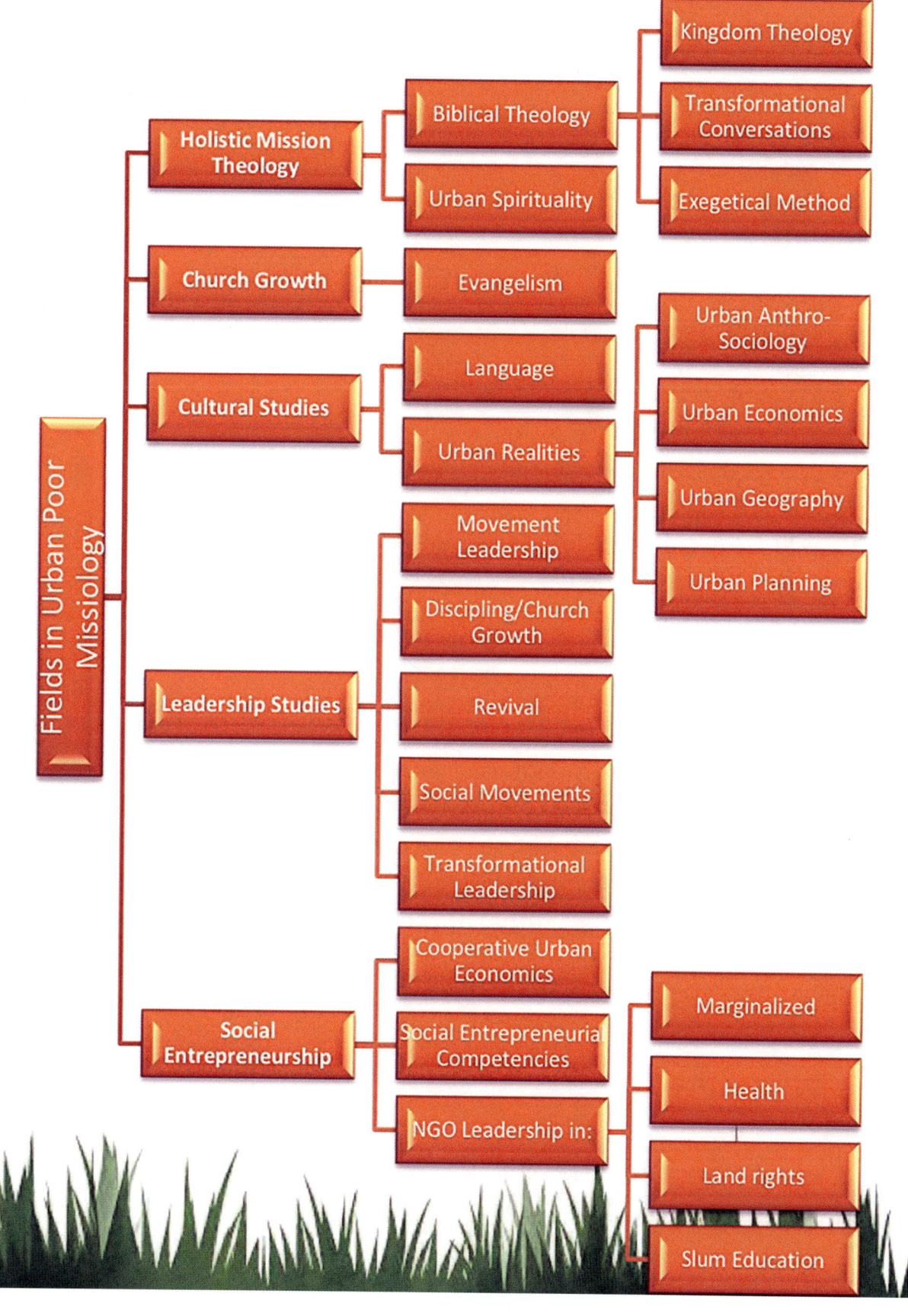

07

A New Field: Urban Poor Movement Leadership

The MATUL focus:

Moving from Leadership to wider Apostolic Leadership

Moving from effective roles among the poor to a breadth of roles

Exploring the progressions from being a leader to becoming a movement leader

Inherent in Jesus' training is the expectation that his disciples would multiply fruit, much fruit. good seed. This defines the core theme of this domain.

> "Unless a grain of wheat falls into the ground and dies it remains alone but if it dies it bears much fruit" (John 12: 24-26).

> "You did not choose me but I chose you that you should go and bear much fruit and that your fruit should abide" (John 15:16).

But it comes as surprise to many of us, that after 20 years ministering we are now leading scores of thousands of people. Somehow we have stumbled into *movement leadership* because we have planted good seed and that good seed keeps multiplying.

This has to do with organic systems in contrast with mechanised production lines. Forests multiply without human energy because God has built that multiplication into the DNA of the trees.

Thus the heart of this degree has to do with moving from a little and poor quality seed sowing to the breadth of planting for harvest and sowing of good seed that has a dynamic life-changing power. This involves progressions from early Leadership fruitfulness to full apostolic Leadership .

> There is an old Persian story of a wise King. In return for great service he offered one of his nobles a choice: to be given a room full of rice, or to be given a grain of rice on the first square of a chess board, 2 on the second, 4 on the third, 8 on the fourth, 16 on ... up to the 64th square. The noble chose the room of rice. Was he wise?

But the seed is not just ideas, it is life transferral and it is life transferral in the midst of death, painful, bloody, dirty, messy, abusive death. Movement Leadership is no flashy Television show, it is a wandering in the midst of poverty. The deeper the death, the greater the harvest.

Thus (a) the power of multiplication inherent in organic growth and (b) the power of quality seed and (c), the depth of its fall into the ground all feed into our coming to a place of leadership of thousands. We then face the question, as God blesses, are we ready for this? In this course we will look at the following:

*M*ovement Leadership Training

*C*hurch-planting Movements

*R*evival Movements

*S*ocial Movements

*C*itywide Transformation Movements

*H*olistic Urban Poor Church-planting Movements

In the first course on a *Biblical Theology, of Urban Mission*, each week students have to go out into the community and talk to the people about how they see community issues - for example if studying Exodus, they need to go and ask people about how they feel about the laws for the poor. Then they have to relate it in the conversation to what they have been studying in the scriptures. Each week they begin to relate more of the scriptures. Evangelism then becomes natural to them as they converse with people about good news for their daily issues.

In the *Building Faith Communities* course they have to learn a second skill, how to gather people into a small group to study the scriptures. Those who can form groups can form movements. It is an essential skill . In the *Movement Leadership* course they have to multiply these cells (Diagram on next page).

Thus, three courses focus the degree. But this is in the context of poverty, so church-planting must engage holistically, 7 courses develop social entrepreneurship responses, and five internships and one course also may also be described as community transformation content.

And he gave some to be apostles, some prophets, some evangelists, some pastors and teachers, to prepare God's people for works of service, so that the body of Christ may be built up (Eph 4:11,12).

The books *Companion to the Poor* (Grigg, 2014) and *Cry of the Urban Poor* (Grigg 2004) are central to the degree in the *Building Faith Communities* course and lay out the patterns and framework of holistic urban poor church-planting.

Core missiological principles are examined in the *Biblical Theology of Urban Missions* in the sections on Jesus' discipling patterns, the movement multiplication principles (church growth principles) in the book of Acts, and the leadership development principles in the epistles.

Movement Leadership

Prior Learning
The course is built on prior learning in earlier courses (TUL 505, 520, 530): issues in incarnational leadership; leadership in multiple phases of life; development of apostolic, prophetic, evangelistic and diaconal (630) leadership in emerging churches; identification and development of personal spiritual Leadership gifts; relationship of poverty to leadership emergence; women and family issues in leadership, community organizing (655).

Church Growth/Revival Movement Leadership
These are in the context of church growth theories (McGavran, 1970, not later version, Hesselgrave 1987, Garrison, 1999, Schwartz, 1996), These theories are examined from urban poor leaders case studies.

Anthropological church growth elements (Hiebert, 1995) include processes of multiplying ministries through the training of spiritually-gifted believ-

Without the church-planting courses the MATUL would contract from apostolic training into a community development (diaconal) program, training workers in transfering resources from rich to poor.

ers among the poor; development of apostolic and prophetic leadership; cell multiplication (Neighbour, 1995, DAWN); web movements (Tippett, 1971), people movements (McGavran, 1970 version); revitalization (Wallace, 2003) and revival movements (Snyder, 1997; Grigg, 2009); patterns of urban poor church growth (Grigg, 2004, 2014); ; multiple ethnic styles of leadership and decision-making, contrasting cultural styles between urban managerial styles and lowland peasant/tribal consensus based leadership styles (Hesselgrave 1987; Lynch, c1979); inside and outside leadership styles; diffusion of innovations (Rogers, 2003; and disciples); processes of catalysing indigenous leadership and theologising styles and formation of committed communities (Winters, 1974; Mellis,1976).

Social Movement Theory

Social Movement theory has its roots in anthropological studies on charisma (Weberian school); cultural roles and movements (Gerlach & Hine, 1970; Hoffer, 1951); educational theses (Friere, 1986; Alinsky, 1969) developed by Salvatierra (2014) on community organisation. We examine Maslow (1954) and other psychological theories on the implications of hierarchies of needs on urban poor leadership emergence.

Theory of Citywide Networking

Partnerships (Butler, Garvin, 1998) and networking in bringing about citywide spiritual and social change (Grigg, 2007, 2009), are examined in case studies of bringing about unity and prayer movements in global cities. We examine theory and models from multiple cities of the mobilisation of city-wide prayer and ethnic reconciliation processes (Dawson, 1996a, 1996b). Spiritual leadership is in the context of cities and spiritual powers (Silvoso, 1994; Aldrich, 1992).

From Revival to Social Movements

Part of this course is the dialogue on how churches create leadership that then engage in the public domain, and seeking correlation of principles between revival movements and social movements (Grigg, 2010).

The seed is not money, the seed is the gospel. The gospel of the Kingdom generates transformation.

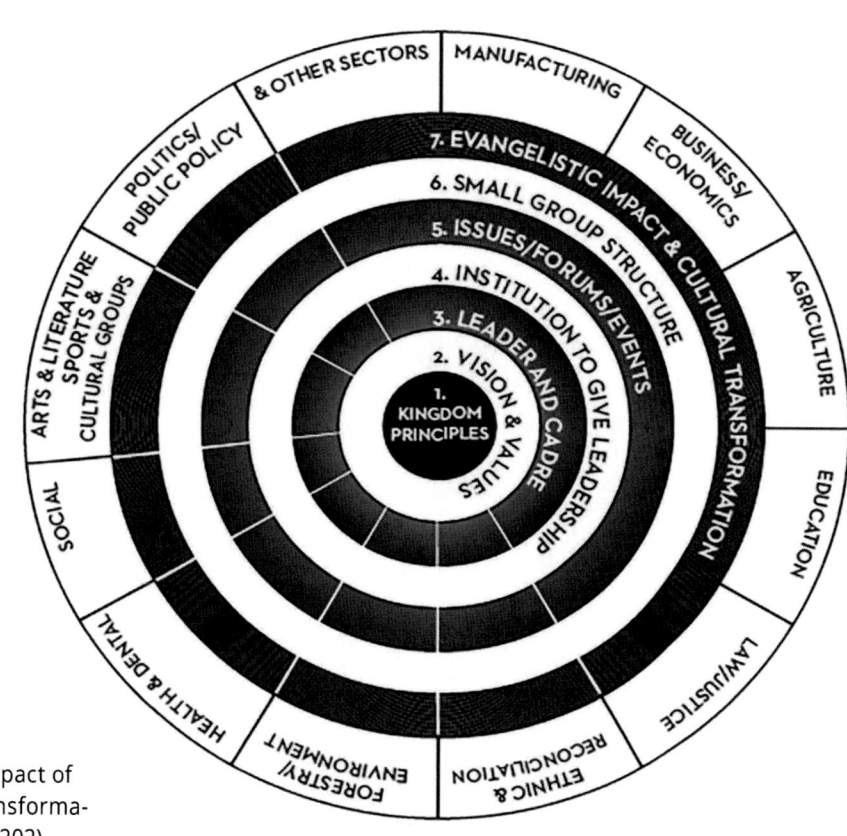

Model for structuring impact of revival movements on transformation of cities (Grigg, 2009: 202)

Progressions from Religious to Social Movements

Urban Spirituality Course

- The beginning of bearing fruit is incarnational living

Biblical Theology of Urban Mission Course

- Principles of discipling, revival and church growth movement multiplication in Jesus and Acts

Building Faith Communities Course

- Incarnation provides the context for evangelism
- Evangelism provides the content of small group formation
- Small group multiplication leads to church-planting

Movement Leadership Course

- Multiplying churches requires apostolic leadership (Movement Leadership course)
- Healthy churches result in revival movements

Social Entrepreneurship and Community Development Courses

- Leadership in churches leads to holistic engagement by deacons

Movement Leadership, Advocacy Courses

- Engaged leaders spawn social movements

Extended Family Bible Study

Diagram: the progressions of Transformative Revival: from the falling of the Spirit on groups to cultural renewal. If there is a response by the culture to cultural revitalization (Grigg 2009).

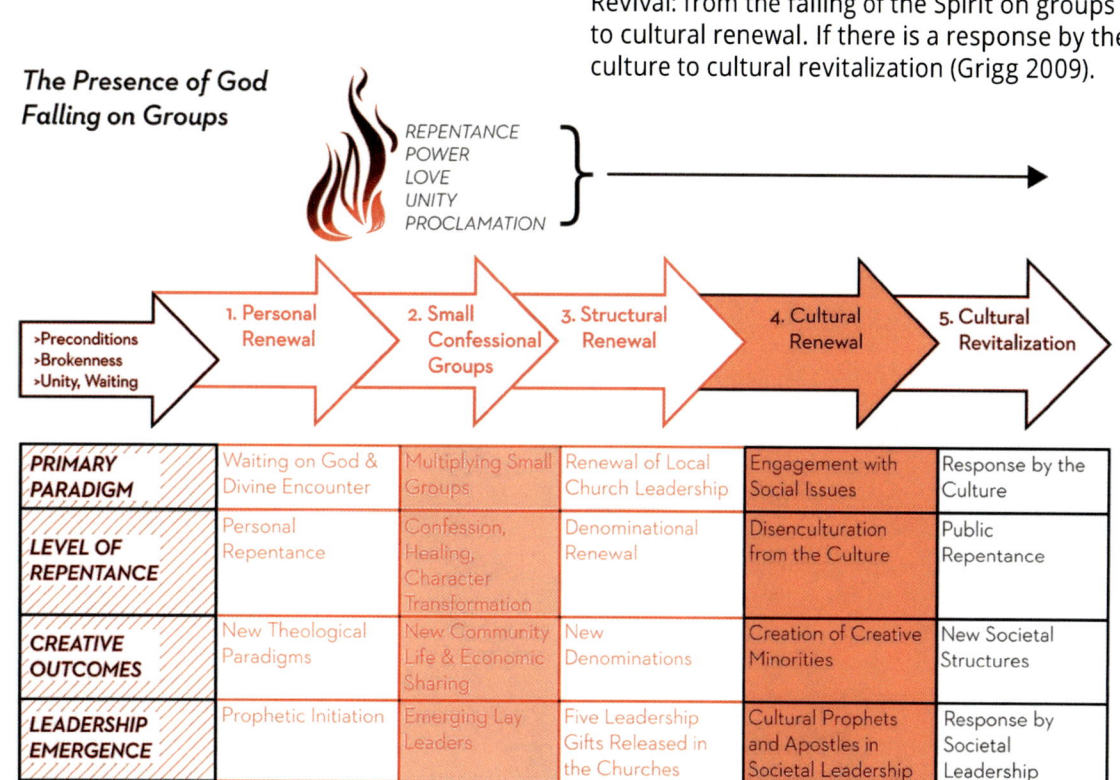

The Presence of God Falling on Groups

REPENTANCE
POWER
LOVE
UNITY
PROCLAMATION

> Preconditions
> Brokenness
> Unity, Waiting

	1. Personal Renewal	2. Small Confessional Groups	3. Structural Renewal	4. Cultural Renewal	5. Cultural Revitalization
PRIMARY PARADIGM	Waiting on God & Divine Encounter	Multiplying Small Groups	Renewal of Local Church Leadership	Engagement with Social Issues	Response by the Culture
LEVEL OF REPENTANCE	Personal Repentance	Confession, Healing, Character Transformation	Denominational Renewal	Disenculturation from the Culture	Public Repentance
CREATIVE OUTCOMES	New Theological Paradigms	New Community Life & Economic Sharing	New Denominations	Creation of Creative Minorities	New Societal Structures
LEADERSHIP EMERGENCE	Prophetic Initiation	Emerging Lay Leaders	Five Leadership Gifts Released in the Churches	Cultural Prophets and Apostles in Societal Leadership	Response by Societal Leadership

08

While the essential dynamic that transforms is the expansion of the work of the Holy Spirit in revival and church-planting movements, that Holy Spirit is also the one who formed the creation. He is an economic and environmental Spirit.

Contextual theology for urban poor people involves responses to poverty. The starting point for this are the many Biblical principles of economic discipleship. Teaching principle of creativity, productivity, thrift, management leads to increased success in entrepreneurship among poor people.

As Christians in the community they also have a concern about peoples health, education, garbage, housing, so take lead in community organizing to accomplish goals in such arenas. This social entrepreneurship requires a development of skill-sets of resource raising, people management, financial management, board and leadership skills, business planning, fund-raising.

7 of the courses in the MATUL lend themselves to training some of these skills. The starting point is in the Community Economics course which covers ten Biblical principles, and explores these at individual, community, city and national/international levels, looking at cooperative schemes and micro-finances.

Five internships where students are working within NGO's gives them inside understandings of NGO management, funding, financial management, budgeting, boards, etc. The community transformation course involves

A New Field in (Slum) Social Entrepreneurship

Lower Circuit Economy to Upper Circuit Entrepreneurship

them in the logistics of a seed project with a local church.

These are integrated in the *Organizational And Entrepreneurial Leadership* course which step by step leads them to develop a business plan, financial plans, funding plan, personnel plan for a local organization, ideally where the plan is good enough so that a funder invests small capital.

Thus graduates should:

- Have understanding or skills and philosophy of social entrepreneurship for starting NGO's or churches,.
- Know how to screen and facilitate community members in their entrepreneurship or in social entrepreneurship. They should be familiar with the complete range of skills for managing such processes.
- Know how to move into business, but with a social conscience.
- Some will move into the global social entrepreneurial scene as businessmen /women or as leaders in large multinational NGO's.
- Have intimate knowledge of urban poor contextual dynamics.

| colspan table | | | | |

Ten Principles of Economic Discipleship

Principle	Genesis	Jubilee	Gospels & Acts	Epistles
1. The Worth and Dignity of each Individual	Created in God's image		Care for the lame, blind, needy, widows	Core for widows, orphans
2. Creativity	God the creator			Spirit sets free
3. Productivity	Good outcomes	6yrs and 49 yrs of productivity	Parables of multiplying seed as a Kingdom principle	
4. Cooperative Economics	Let "us" make		Common purse, Not a needy one among them	Provide for others
5. Work & Rest	He makes He structures God rests, Sabbath rest	Sabbath, Jubilee rest	Jubilee come Labour in the gospel	Work with hands (1 Thes 4:11), provide for family and for needy Rest
6. Detachment & Simplicity				
7. Redistribut'n for Equality	Abraham tithes	Jubilee –return of land	No needy one Weekly Giving	Global redist'n (2 Cor 8,9) Role of a Deacon
8. Management, Savings &	Manage the Earth, Jubilee cancels debts	Land needs rest	Parables of Stewardship, Debts cancelled	Owe no person, Simplicity
9. Celebration	It was good	Blow trumpet	Worship daily	
10. Land & Property Rights	Each family to own their own Home (including Levites)	Each family to be given back land All to own	Forsake all, yet own home	Provide for Family (1 Tim 5:8)

Chart: Ten economic principles underlying the degree, developed in Kiwinomics

*I*s the Kingdom Directional?

*T*he movement leadership course and the social entrepreneurship courses expand ministry leadership dynamics. This is complemented by the emphasis within courses on administrative leadership and working with the structures of NGO's. This overcomes are the practical results of a theological division between two views of the Kingdom, two views of holistic ministry and two sets of giftings. I will contrast these as the apostolic and the diaconal views of the Kingdom.

Theology: **Apostolic movements** understand the coming of the Kingdom is through the advances of the preached gospel, which is then outworked in discipleship in the local churches. **Development agencies,** often by governmental controls do not highly prioritize proclamation but seek holistic engagement with issues that cause poverty.

Understanding of Goal and Process: **Apostolic movements** see the expansion of the church and its engagement with the community as the core of bringing about godly leadership who can bring change. Poverty change is not their primary focus, but one of the aspects of the Kingdom transformation of their people. In contrast, **development agencies** largely see wealth transferral as the essential response to differences between rich and poor. Their objectives tend to be delivery of projects among the poor as the means of changing poverty. I call the first directional holism, built around the evangelism, and the second round holism where all things including evangelism are equal (see diagram).

Giftedness: **Church-planting movements** are lead by apostle and prophets and evangelists. **NGO leadership** requires high levels of administration skills, and so are lead by those with diaconal giftings.

People vs. Place: **Apostolic movements** (Church growth studies) focus on people development and sociological momentum. Deacons were appointed subsequent to the formation of the early church. Their role is subject to the apostolic leadership. **Community development** focuses on the holism of place.

Since both have their roots in the scriptures, it is important to understand the differences, affirm the giftings, and seek to work for the common good by understanding how these complement each other. The MATUL trains people according to their call and gifting, so some pursue the apostolic call, and some the diaconal calling of NGO's.

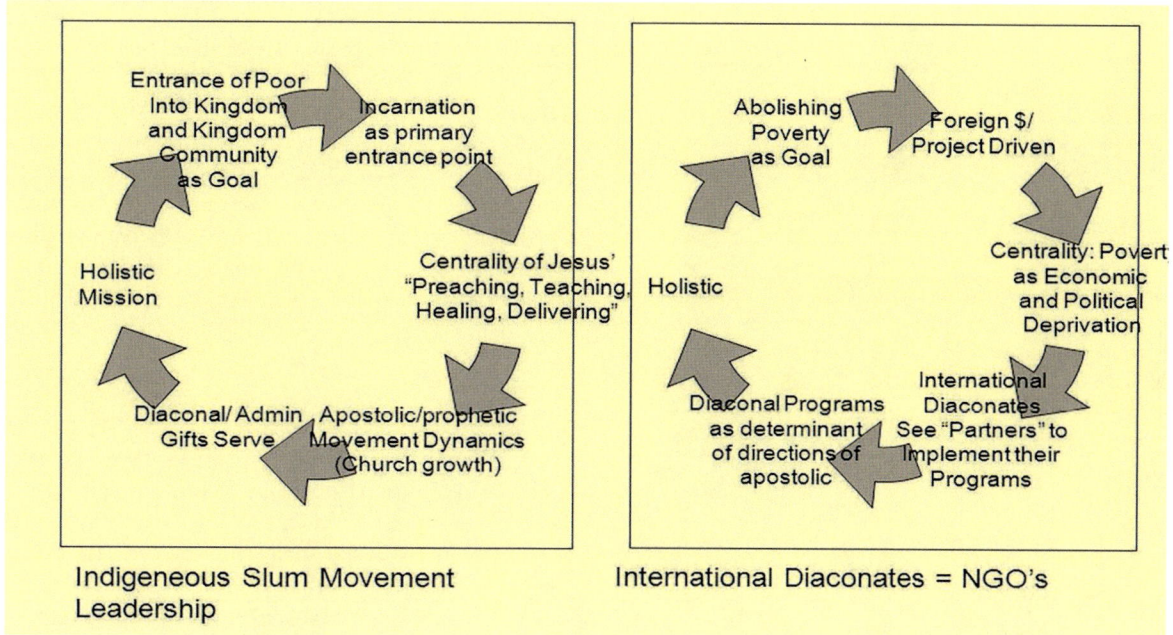

Diagram: Contrast between two versions of holistic Kingdom mission: The Biblical model of Kingdom development and the role of deacons in the international development industry transferring wealth.

09

New Field: Urban Poor Spirituality

We have integrated a new academic field of Urban Poor Spirituality within the slums.

It becomes a field within Urban Poor Missiology

It becomes a course within the MATUL degree.

Incarnation or *solidarity* are terms we use. *Justice* is central to our conversation. We see the gospel as engaging city *structures*. We *share the pain*, and many have been *set free* from deep levels of sin, addiction, criminality. Our theologizing is by means of *story* (which I cover elsewhere in Transformational Conversations), which includes a high value on *listening and learning in humility*. We think in terms of *movements and social change* so the God of our spirituality is a *God of action* (more than Aquinas' static God of being) and *multi-ethnicity* more than traditions. We are *boundary-crossers*, and eclectic, but *seeking identity* is part of that *journey*. We are open to *diversity*, celebrate diversity, and affirm cultural differences.

We are *urban workers*. And we are deeply spiritual. But our spirituality is distinct. It is urban spirituality.

The Nature of Urban Spirituality

Professors have a great deal of flexibility in teaching content in their courses. And to teach a course in Urban Spirituality, a professor likely has done their doctorate that includes courses in spirituality, and is involved in an urban ministry. The following is a description of the conceptualization of the field of urban spirituality, submitted with respect, hoping to steer expertise but not limit it. Urban Spirituality is a distinct field in its own right, so it is important that the core of that field be transmitted to students not courses in ancient monastic spirituality.

How can we say it is a field? Because when we are with other urban workers we immediately sense that kinship of spirit, that camaraderie that contains some underlying commitments. Our discussion is sprinkled with some core terms or values that are part of our common understanding – and that is also our experience globally. There are other areas where we don't quite understand each others' traditions or experiences so we listen and learn – these we may define as secondary terms or values -they likely don't define the field. Commonalities define a field.

Structuring Urban Spirituality Content

Spirituality is a big term. We are from an evangelical Christian tradition, so it is not Buddhist mantras.

A course in urban spirituality thus explores the development of Christian urban spiritualities, as well as the skills of leading spiritual formation among the urban poor. It will include a personal inventory of character, calling, and giftedness and addresses human development and family life in the slum context.

Course Rationale

Relationship to Rest of Program: Well developed inner spirituality and knowledge of the work of the Holy Spirit and the ability to train others in areas of spirituality is a prerequisite for sustained ministry among the needy. Life within high-stress urban contexts requires a transcendent source of hope, emotional and psychological balance, a centeredness in the love of God and expressing that love – all of which are undergirded by a spiritually disciplined life. The course on Church-planting requires leading people to Christ and discipling them, essentially the arenas of justification and sanctification. The course on movements leadership expands the concept of calling and directionality from within the urban spirituality course.

Historic Spirituality Framework: The first classes are simply identifying what is Christian spirituality, justification, sanctification, and the work of the Spirit in historic Christianity and more particularly in evangelical Christian theology. Evangelical theology was birthed in the revivals of the reformation – the pietists, the Wesleyan revival, the 1st and second Great Awakenings, all experiencing the falling of the Holy Spirit on great masses of people, so we are within a tradition, not of purely academic spirituality of a belief system, but of experiential spirituality interpreted by theology.

Spirituality from the Holy Spirit: Christian spirituality can be taught centered around doctrine, disciplines, psychological approaches or the work of the Holy Spirit. Evangelical spirituality has always centered in movements of revival of the Holy Spirit vs. the more psychological approaches derived from Catholicism or psychotherapy. There are elements of each in this course. In this course, the class seeks to move into dimensions of the work of the Holy Spirit.

Sensitive contrast of the diversity of doctrinal approaches about activity of the Spirit needs be developed in a way that diverse traditions in the class are not offended. One of the goals of this class is that each student can freely move in the power of the Spirit, hear his voice, and exercise appropriately their spiritual gifts, in ways that maintain harmony of the Spirit across the body of Christ.

Lecturers and supporting faculty need to be aware that this may also provoke some degree of spiritual warfare during this training. It would be wise for this course to always be team taught by people both academically learned and practically experienced in these areas of releasing people from sin and bondages into the fullness of the work of the Spirit).

Spirituality as God Engaging our Human Spirits - Self Awareness: Knowing our own spirits or self-knowledge is part of historic Catholic and Presbyterian Christianity. Catholicism has resisted the direct interventions of revival, so has been forced to define spirituality in terms of the human spirit, and academics. Self-understanding in the course involves psychological testing, a test in cross-cultural abilities, Strengsthsfinder, and a gifts test.

Spirituality begins in brokenness at the Cross, so early in the course, (usually the third or fourth week), we deal with trauma, brokenness, pain, illness, sinful habits. This is the week that begins most on the spiritual journey of healing through the program. We cannot, as professors deal with deeper psychological issues or pastoral issues, so some find counsellors, some we refer, etc.

This is not a counselling course, but in this first semester, it also enables screening candidates for suitability for ministry in areas of family, psychological, emotional and spiritual wholeness and hence enables pastoral care for problem areas such as compulsive sin, demonic possession, areas of bondage (which may be to leadership, narrow doctrinal bondage, work expectations within their mission, family bondages, paranoias etc.).

Apostolic or Cross-Cultural Spirituality

This also enables evaluation of the candidate's spiritual maturity potential to fulfil the outcomes required for the whole program and fit for urban ministry. I used to teach this section at the end but have found that these issues when broached early, open up deep areas that during the remainder of the course, the student can engage with appropriate support structures.

If people should be in cross-cultural ministry, we need to examine cross-cultural spiritualities in multiple ways. First, their capacity. Then exploring the spirituality of their forefathers, so in a class with German descent, Hispanic descent, Indian descent etc., there may emerge some interesting reflections on how they genetically respond to God and the work of the Spirit – and of different cultural phenomenology, and how their communities respond.

Facilitators should sit at least twice with each person during the first Modules in a process of evaluation with them outside of the classroom time, based on some of the above questionnaires they do and working with them on defining a program for spiritual growth. This introductory course should also facilitate them into a relationship with a spiritual director for the remainder of the two-year program.

For those going overseas cross-culturally, there is a requirement that they go through psychological and medical prefield screening, as the basis of "confirmation to proceed" to the field. This is undertaken by their mission sending organizations.

Urban Poor Spirituality

This is a course on urban poor spiritualities (a largely uncharted academic area) not a traditional course on classic Western or Catholic spiritual exercises (though these are a significant section of the course). Because it is uncharted, the course participants themselves need to be encouraged through a storytelling approach to inject their knowledge of urban poor spirituality into the course processes. Attending urban poor churches gives entrance to these dimensions. Urban poor spiritualities are very different from classical Western spiritualities or even much evangelical spirituality (See Cry of the Urban Poor, chaps. 15,16 for anthropological reasons for this).

Such urban poor spirituality revolves around the Holy Spirit in the community of faith (vs the individualism and quietness of the leisured classes). It is noisy, emotional, involves frequent power encounters and healing of devastating emotional problems often taking many years, under authoritarian leadership. Engaging these issues of urban poor spirituality and relating these cultural characteristics to ancient Western or more middle-class traditions is a critical part of the course, leaving the learners with a mindset of openness to understand instead of shock at difference.

On the other hand, Pentecostal pastors from among the urban, the poor and the working classes will be expanding their understanding to see the whole field of spirituality as a critical element for long-term wholeness. Classic spiritual disciplines are critical for their survival and also critical for middle class students who are entering urban poor ministry in the class to cope with the stresses of incarnational ministry. In this we draw from the experience of the leaders of emergent Protestant apostolic orders with whom I have had the privilege of being among.

Spiritual Disciplines

Classical Spiritual Disciplines: Reflections on the continuity of building an intimate relationship with God in the context of the city, knowing the appropriate use and application of prayer and fasting, encountering and responding to spiritual conflict, exercising deliverance ministry, in-depth bible study, practicing the presence of God, the exercise of spiritual gifts with an attitude of servanthood, and practicing moral integrity and ethics may all be part of those disciplines.

Urban Spirituality Disciplines for Relocators: But what are the distinct urban spirituality disciplines? the disciplines of the urban poor? and the disciplines of those who work among the urban poor?

The latter is developed in my *Lifestyle and Values of Servants* (1981), and developed by some of the apostolic urban poor missions that have emulated what we did with their ownl ifestyle commitments: Incarnation, Community, Simplicity, Voluntary Poverty Evangelism, Doing Justice, Development, Work and Rest, Joy in Suffering, etc. They then develop their own *Rule of Life* for the next two years in the program.

Slum Church Disciplines: The disciplines that work among *urban poor pastors and churches* are well defined, and international, but very different to that of relocators. The culture of poverty defines them (I develop this in *Cry of the Urban Poor*, Chap 16). It is communal , so church is nearly every day. It engages the spirit world. It is deeply emotional as people are dealing with deep pain. It is oral, so story based and preaching is from story to story: the story of the community to the parallel Biblical stories. Worship invokes the presence of the SPirit and his presecince falls on people and touches their wounds. There is much lament. There is regular rhythm in services...

I personally go deeper into some disciplines like the

nature of the ministry of intercession, and all through, I train in scripture memory- essential as a number will likely spend years in prison in the future (we also discuss martyrdom as a grace), then a guided retreat or a silent retreat in the city. Atty. Raineer Chu of Manila has found the idea of silent retreat so powerful that he frames a section of the course around it and his order, *Companions with the Poor,* practice this regularly with great impact.

Justice Spirituality

This is a whole new concept to many, so it requires time to be introduced to its disciplines – this is expanded in the courses on Advocacy and Movement Leadership.

For relocators, it is a central component of their lifestyle, this walking in repentance, and humility, asking forgiveness for past wrongs done by majority cultures in exploiting indigenous cultures, directing righteous anger into reconciliatory change and seeking restitution.

There are various strands to a very broad topic: those of the community organizers fighting against injustice from outside the system using people power. Alexia Salvatierra (2014) has beautifully captured the necessary spirituality.

The spirituality of the academe expressed in Postcolonial theology and its analysis of historical injustices, and creating the polemic for rectification and restitution is different. A long hard road of study, thought, wisdom and engaging with leadership of peoples and nations (Tizon, 2018 ch 3)

In a parallel field, Glen Stassen identifies *Ten Practices of Just Peacemaking* (2008). These are activist definitions of being and doing, not inner values. James K Smith goes into a different set of values in interweaving religion, ritual, and worship into the complexity of the public sphere (2017). Gustavo Gutierrez (1984) explores the same dynamics from within oppressed peoples applying liberation theology to develop a Catholic liberation spirituality.

Economic spirituality is mentioned but is better developed in the Community Economics class - Christian spirituality is not Buddhist nor gnostic, but rooted in dirt under one's fingernails, for from dust we came. I cover ten values in *Kiwinomics* (2017). Every other course has its own derived spirituality, so the faculty who teaches the initial course has to work with each other faculty to consider how spirituality can be devel-oped across the degree.

Phenomenology of the Holy Spirit

Phenomenology: At various points the nature of the spirit world surfaces, as the historic warfare between Spirit and the World, the flesh and the devil is discussed. At some point, it is important in urban poor spirituality to deal with the nature of the demonic, of deliverance and of wider dimensions of spiritual warfare. The poor dwell in a spirit-filled world of dwarfs and spirits and powers.

Based on the theology of the Holy Spirit and the phenomenology and liturgy of their traditions, this opens discussions on how the Spirit engages people though the mind, the emotions, and physically, depending on culture, personality and tradition.

Cultural Spiritualities and Phenomenology: That discussion prepares them for interpreting in their new culture from their old tradition. It begins their capacity to explain in different terms the new phenomenology without losing their mind. (This is crucial pre-field or first semester training but it is not a full cross-cultural course). When people are overwhelmed with the person of the Holy Spirit, how are they culturally wired to respond? Each culture is different. The phenomenology of revival is different. Each student is asked to find five articles about spirituality in that culture - this begins them on a pilgrimage of understanding.

Spirituality and Marriage: Issues of sustaining and developing a healthy marriage partnership in the midst of the stresses of urban ministry and poverty are briefly engaged in the light of contextual spirituality. For single people, similarly, issues of developing a godly singleness are touched on. This is delicate. If there are single women in the course it is wiser for an experienced cross-cultural woman worker to teach this topic – men really have little idea of the issues, and one word spoken in error can create enormous waves in such a sensitive topic. The spirituality of marriage and singleness opens up new dimensions, and often deep childhood or college year trauma, so making sure adequate connections to counsellors to whom they can be connected is important. One assignment that has become a favourite is for married couples to take their wives out for a meal to discuss how the spiritual development of their marriage.

Timing and Spirituality

I use a framework of the Four Seasons of Christian growth (Grigg, 2004, ch. 13), in one's own life and the lives of a churches, ascertaining which season each person is in and how that contributes to their spiritual development and function within a ministry team or faith community. There are many other frameworks in terms of lifelong spirituality and its seasons, so the course becomes an introduction to some of these. The Tonna-Hall inventory[21] is perhaps the most comprehensive integration of the various theories on values as life progresses based on the psychological, educational and spiritual theories underlying human development. Values are central to an understanding of the human dimension of the human-divine interaction we identify as spirituality.

Practicum

In the practical phase of the course above, students are invited, through spiritual direction, personal journaling and group interaction:

- to explore the nature of one's spiritual formation
- to experiment with a variety of spiritual practices that encourage a contemplative approach to life
- to share one's experience of these practices in a community setting
- to integrate academic and professional foundations around a center of spiritual maturity in Christ
- to examine traditional Christian practice in the light of a commitment to social justice
- to identify core idols and life patterns needing repentance, spiritual healing, and transformation
- to nurture a "rule of life" that can sustain one's witness within slum environments

Retreats: Field instructors draw upon spiritual formation resources and local retreat facilities to organize 1-2 day-long retreats. Students come to these retreats prepared to share out of their spiritual journals. These journals record responses to various Self-Examination Questions, Notes that they have developed on Filipino (or Tamil or Maori) Spirituality or Slum Spirituality, and Reflections on Leadership of a small group in spiritual growth – personal life reflections that can contribute to the fashioning of a rich group life and enable students to appreciate how God is forming them through individual and interpersonal experience, nature, and the urban systems in which they live and work.

Urban Poor Churches: 1-2 visits to urban poor churches of another tradition takes them across barrier in real time, facilitating interpretation between the theology of these peoples' churches and within their own theology.

Learning Objectives

Thus we have defined a new field of urban poor spirituality for apostles and relocators and a different dynamic for slum-dwellers themselves. Both have a different set of disciplines. References to core texts may be found at the end of this book. The following are some objectives for an urban spirituality course.

1. Defining the Field of Spirituality
- What is Spirituality? Specifically Christian spirituality? and evangelical Christian spirituality?
- What is the aim of spiritual growth? And the methods and practices?
- How do justification and sanctification differ? And what is the role of the Holy Spirit and our human spirits in sanctification? And culture? And poverty?
- How do time, and culture affect the journey? Are there stages? Are these different dependent on our personality, and life experiences and age?

2. Theology of the Holy Spirit
- Understand the relationship of the anointing of the Spirit and ministry among the poor.
- Experience the opportunity in a supportive context for prayer that breaks barriers to the work of the Holy Spirit in each others lives.

3. Grief, Suffering, Pain, Forgiveness and the Cross
- Will understand leading recovery from grief and suffering by approaching their own past.
- Past hurts will be brought before God and where possible, processes for resolution determined.
- Will have been examined a theology of Redemptive Suffering .
- Will have identified and accessed literature on Redemptive Suffering and Dealing with Grief .

4. Apostolic or Cross-Cultural Spirituality
- Understand possible spiritual and emotional dynamics during years of transition cross-culturally.
- Praxis: Have reflected on significant new self-knowledge from a variety of analyses.

5. Evangelical Spirituality
- Understand the nature of evangelicalism
- Understand classic evangelical commitments to methodological engagement with the word and prayer and a regular discipline of life

6. Vocational Spirituality
- Evaluate motivations, emotional fitness, habits,

personality dynamics and character preparation for urban ministry.

- Begin to think through directional spirituality through developing a personal Lifestyle and Values document.

7.Urban Poor Spirituality

- Develop an understanding of essential characteristics of urban poor culture and identify derivative characteristics of spirituality.
- Extended a theological framework for encountering the miraculous in ministry.

8. Justice Spirituality

- Understand a diversity of strands of Christian justice spirituality.
- Understand the relationship of the three main traditions of spiritual growth in urban poor ministry in the context of injustice.
- Evaluate the effectiveness of spiritual disciplines in enabling you to cope with the pressures of urban life in the midst of injustice.

10. Indigenous Spirituality

- Become sensitive to the different cultural starting points and emphases in the emergence of a culturally relevant spirituality;
- Learn some initial patterns of discerning the core

values of the culture and their affect on spirituality.

11. Incarnational Spirituality

- Analyze the nature of lifestyle, value and ministry commitments that can be renewed yearly to enable sustained living among the poor.
- Define a framework for evaluating spirituality in relationship to wealth, poverty and simplicity.

12. Urban Spirituality

- Understand the context of urban poor spirituality and be able to analyze expected types of spirituality the context causes or requires;
- Be able to evaluate the effectiveness of our spiritual disciplines in enabling us to cope with the pressures of urban life.

13. Family/ Singleness Spirituality

- Reflect on issues that need to be addressed in sustaining a healthy family life when living and ministering among the poor.
- Understand the effect of stress on spirituality and family.

14. Confronting the Spirit World

- An academic framework is presented that enables discernment and wise engagement against the spirit world.

Slum Pastors at Worship, Hyderabad

Part 4: INNOVATIVE EDUCATION

10 Vocational Training Models

The Idea of VET

Having defined the philosophy of education, the style of learning in the domain, it may be obvious that the MATUL in many ways follows the model of Vocational Training Courses or what is known as VET in some countries - Vocation Education and Training.

It is based on the concept of apprenticeship. Most courses involve on-the-job training under the leadership of an experienced worker.

There is a sense of excellence in VET training. A master builder is a master at his craft. Vocational Training prepares people for their work. While the MATUL creates reflective space for leaders to think philosophically, each course also has a skills outcome.

Each has a clear sense of the outcomes - what jobs people are being trained for. Competencies define the outcome of courses. Assessment is based on criteria for each of these competencies. "What is different between countries is how competency-based standards are conceptualized, who and by whom they are developed, and the degree to which standards shape curriculum and assessment" (Boud, p. 181).

Skills are transferred, but also a value system, a sense of identity, a sense of place within a vocation. These are very human dynamics, often only transferred one-on-one.

Time frames are defined. Each vocation understands the time it takes to learn the whole field, and the progressions within that time frame.

Labour is usually exchanged for education. It is a trade-off. The labour is productive during the training, but may not be expert - that depends on the expertise of the master supervisor.

Several different models each have made contributions to the overall idea:

Apprenticeships

Skills in a specific industry (and often high level skills) are transferred though initial classroom training, then on-the- job mentoring with a master tradesman, supplemented by block courses related to specific technical components of the job. This tends to be formalized training, recognized by a guild or association in its speciality.

On the Job Training

This tends to be less formal than an apprenticeship and in reality occurs in all businesses and workplaces to some extent. It is usually non-formal and generally does not indicate formal courses.

Manpower Training

The terminology is relatively new but the process is as

old as history. Perhaps there is a need in a certain city for many workers to finish a certain project. There is excess (and hence cheap) labour in another city. How can these be trained to migrate and fill these jobs, remitting back to their poorer community the wealth earned?.

One of our MATUL students studied the training of concrete workers for malls in Brazil. The need was great, but those with some training and knowledge would go to the head of the queue when employment was offered.

This is less formal than an apprenticeship. Less complex training. Short time frame, Specific type of job.

Internships

Internships tend to be from one semester to a year long. A student works with an organization within a specific discipline, based on a contract between student, organization and educational provider. This involves defined learning outcomes, The productive work generally covers the cost of the training input from the organization. The organization gets a free or cheap worker. The learner grows in skill.

This is less personalized than an apprenticeship. Shorter. Practicum tend to be mini internships. Shorter. Less focussed.

The quality of such internships can vary dramatically. Matching student and opportunity is the students responsibility but also requires a skilled educator to evaluate the opportunity and to make sure learning is occurring.

We require each student to interview three organizations and then document the opportunity in each, before deciding which organization. They then have to negotiate how their work will contribute to the organization and what they will learn in return. The organization has to have the capacity to supervise. Often they appear to have, but the director over summer is out for six weeks perhaps, and nothing happens. So a skilled faculty needs to be in personal contact with that leadership and the student to make sure such negotiations end up with a positive context and outcomes. At the end the students write up becomes a significant part of the evaluation as does the evaluation of the student by the supervisor, and the visit by the faculty to the organization to get feedback directly from the director.

This kind of education is generally not part of majority world educational practice, so training of faculty, directors and deans is needed.

Over time, a list of ideal places for internships in a city gets developed.

The MATUL has chosen to go the way of internships, but graduates consistently are asking for more of a consistent apprenticeship model, where they can track through with one discipline across the degree. The initial design works well with young folks who do not know what they wish to focus on. It still can have a focus in one of the semesters on an internship in their chosen field then two research courses with that same organization, so half of the full-time degree is focussed.

But for older workers, their direction tends to be set. Developing a learning contract with them seems to be a wiser way to go, where within the entry period to the degree they identify their goals and specific courses and independent studies and experiences are defined. .

Academic Mentoring

The fifth descriptor of this kind of mentoring is often ignored and that is academic mentoring over the course of a degree. This deeply human interaction is not generally defined in a professor's job description so tends to receive minimal input. Friendly but not deeply engaged!! Too busy with committees and writing books.

It is best developed from the following perspective on character formation. However it does come to a climax in the two semesters of working with students on their research.

Character and Spiritual Formation

Each course in the MATUL has defined outcomes in terms of the head (academic), the heart (character and spiritual formation), the hands (skills) and the habitat (engagement in community).

Character formation across the degree is the program director's role, though this may be assigned to a faculty. It is difficult for adjunct faculty to carry this as they only teach specified courses, though they can become significant in their engagement with students.

Pre-entry or first semester engagement is the core to this level of input. This begins with a spiritual autobiography from potential students. The interview of one hour is a very significant time to identify core directionalities, levels of damage, and extent of experience.

The psychological testing becomes the next step in confirming these first impressions and usually identifies some deep level trauma or sin that needs engagement. Access to a trained counsellor for many is important at this point. Often that begins in the urban spirituality course where the Catholic concept of spiritual formation (that has also become popular with Presbyterian circles) becomes significant in its understanding of knowing oneself as part of the self-Spirit dynamic. This course leads to a spiritual formation plan. It also often leads to deep encounters with the Holy Spirit, whose presence is the key to deep level healing that counselling can often not touch.

The academics then enable a development of the directionalities, an opening to new dimensions theologically that set many free from the bondage of narrow theological confines in local congregations. Often understanding issues itself is liberating to the Spirit, as Jesus says, "The truth will set you free!"

Creating liberty in each course for students to explore these issues as they arise can be significant. Mentoring throughout the program as to personal styles,, conflicts with people, management, dealing with family issues, grief, are all part of the pastoral professor's role. The university prefers less investment, simply working at the head level because it usually defines academics simply as knowledge. But the scriptures define *the fear of the Lord as the beginning of wisdom*. As such, the MATUL is a wisdom degree.

The lawyers hate such pastoral engagement because it is potentially full of minefields. And they are right. Care must be taken, not to intrude beyond one's skill, capacity and role; to draw on expert counsellors when needed; to be careful in documenting engagements; to consistently have back up from the dean in complex issues; to maintain confidentiality; to recognise that the seminary is not the church, but one small part of people's pilgrimages.

But care does not to ignore the character and spiritual formation. This is a degree in movement leadership. Good seed multiplies. There should not be graduation without character transformation.

Vocational Training Infrastructure

This leads to the critical issue for this study. The outcomes of vocational training are defined by the industry. Industry associations, clusters of leaders within the industry determine these. They set the standards of what is needed to be known. The educational institutions handle the delivery.

Accreditation is thus a dual accreditation - educational quality is managed by the Commission for Higher Education or similar. But credibility of course-work outcomes is handled by the Industry Association. This occurs at low level industry levels such as auto-mechanics but can occur at upper level academic levels as well. Thus the American Psychological Association defines the training psychologists need. The educational institutions develop mechanisms to obtain those outcomes. The Department of Education has requirements for teachers. The academic institutions frame their course designs so that those requirements are met.

Proposal: An Association of Industry Providers

The key to all of this is for the Encarnação Alliance Training Commission to become a Commission of Industry Providers that defines outcomes and credits providers. We expand our network to include leadership and institutions that enable the following:.
• Mass delivery at the grassroots of certificates.
• Integration into recognized diplomas.
• A process where these feed into Bachelor's degrees
• A process where these feed into the MATUL for movement leaders
• A Doctorate in Transformational Urban Leadership by an accredited university.

Proposal: Alternative Credits as an Industry Accreditation Organization.

1. **Mass Delivery of Vocational Training:** At the certificate and diploma level we integrate delivery from multiple sources that meet our criteria for effective slum leader education. Thus, we give credibility to certificates from multiple sources internationally and diplomas where national accreditation processes allow. Four certificates become a diploma recognized by the commission or another body. This follows vocational training models.

2. **High Quality Academic training:** at the MATUL and Doctoral levels we continue to work with existing institutions, who seek accreditation within their own national accreditation systems. This will be with small classes, intensively mentored. The aim is those in movement leadership or moving into movement leadership.

3. **Breadth:** This movement leadership training contin-

ues to cover the six movement leadership roles: apostle, prophet, evangelist, pastor, teacher, deacon/ess (community development worker).

4. *Institutional Requirements:* To be industry recognized, the institutions must be required to meet the requirements for consistent appointment of appropriate leadership and recruiters as part of their professional association obligations (i.e. to remain members they need to fulfil some minimal responsibilities for recruitment, faculty leadership, admin leadership, holistic apostolic movement leadership (vs. community development or social work leadership) and content that meets industry outcomes).

Where is Vocational Training?

That is an interesting question!! it is in the workplace. For the slum pastor that is in the slum. For the slum educator that is in the slum school. AND in the place of reflection - which may be at a training centre, a computer cafe-cum-training centre, or that laptop connected to the internet.

What academic theologians call residency is thus now binary. The Seminary is now in the slums and often in a training centre in the slums or in cyberspace.

Industry Standards Model

Traditional education models repeat what has been taught by previous generations, a body of knowledge with some tweaking. Vocational models may also get locked into an era, thus there are still courses in using sewing machines in many countries, but the model also has the capacity for eternal flexibility. Economic culture changes rapidly. New industries are forming. Each needs to configure an industry-wide approach to training that matches that industry.

Thus urban poor pastoral training is

MATUL: A wisdom degree

not obligated to the formal academic systems of theology but can start with people on the ground.

There is a resistance in academia to education determined by employability. If economics determines educational outcomes, where is the breadth of philosophy and morality needed in liberal education that prepares citizens?

In the MATUL, because each course meshes theology, praxis and social analysis, this criticism is overcome. Theology requires engaging with the philosophy of the course.

Similarly we have laid out the degree with outcomes defined in four dimensions: Head, Heart, Hands and Habitat. - The conceptual/philosophical; the character/spirituality; the skills and the engagement with the community.

Provided administration do not start reducing these down for managerial purposes, these enable both the liberal education of discussion on goals, values, philosophy and the practical skills formation.

Credibility

But it does need to have validity, which includes quality training, clear outcomes and credibility to organizations within the sector. Some structure, and some credibility is needed. Often governments regulate these.

Outcome-Based Education

The above requires definition of the outcomes by the industry are often called standards. These are important at both a degree level (Program Learning Outcomes, (PLO's)) and at a course level (Student Learning Outcomes (SLO's)). There is extensive literature on the philosophy and practice of this approach to education.[22].

The 432 initial outcomes underlying the MATUL came from urban poor workers. They have been refined into about 150 course outcomes from all the courses as the academics have tried to structure. This is mostly positive but schools have a habit of appointing deans with no experience in slum ministry. These have a habit of reducing outcomes to four per course for management purposes. The quality is gone - deans are primarily tasked with sustaining academic quality!!!

This is a conundrum in the design process. One has to differentiate between the required (perhaps 8-12) outcomes of a course defined by the industry and the reduced (4-5) management outcomes which need to be measured for educational validation and make sure that both are sustained.

Similarly new adjuncts come in, and presume they should simply teach what they know, not what a course outline defines. Much is lost. Adjunct mentoring is thus an essential requirement for each program director. Commission videos on the content of each course are a priority need, with a mandate for Directors and Deans also to review them and make sure incoming adjuncts are trained through them.

There has been considerable debate about standards-based education over the decades. The idea promises clarity, precision of outcomes. Advocates argue that traditional teaching approaches are broad and vague in their aims, and that they focus on what knowledge teachers and trainers will try to teach, not what students need to learn. Critics argue that they seek to make simple, what is complex. The outcomes of an educational process cannot all be predetermined. Early attempts to apply this idea in minute details in education reflected *Behavorism* as a philosophy at its worst. Even if teachers could tick off the many criteria, it did not necessarily make them good teachers.

Work Integrated Learning

The more recent movement has been called workplace learning. The Australians have launched a whole new discipline on this with a *Work-based Learning* Journal, The professor's job is to shift from the real-life problems to the expert approaches to solving these problems, to move from specific to the generic.

The idea of becoming the master has evolved to the concept of becoming an expert, to develop expertise. But students do not begin as masters, so development of beginner learning skills in their discipline is needed.

The focus in the MATUL program on internship courses and action-based courses provides a good balance of workplace engagement with conceptual analysis. In the course on *Developing Slum Schools,* for example, is the requirement to work with the administration of a school in the slums in a self-assessment process. This advances the student's skill in administration, and their ability to analyse a school against theoretical constructs.

Examination of both process and outcome also seems necessary for most courses. Thus both the analysis of an internship process, the weekly engagement is necessary, but also an evaluation by the student of their learning outcomes measured against the course student learning outcomes (SLO's).

Lifelong Learning

Lifelong learning can be defined as the "ongoing, voluntary, and self-motivated" pursuit of knowledge for either personal or professional reasons. Therefore, it not only enhances social inclusion, active citizenship, and personal development, but also self-sustainability, as well as competitiveness and employability.

It is usually used in reference to post-formal education. In our context of urban poor leadership the felt needs have to do with identity, credibility, personal effectiveness, as well as financial self-sustainability and effective church growth.

The self sustainability motivation means community engagement while initially an altruistic commitment to implementing truth, is eventually evaluated by pastors for its effectiveness in increasing the tithing congregation's capacity. For the pastor's financial base is the local congregation. For others, it is in capacity to access resources from non-profits or obtain work with a non-profit agency. The margin of error is narrow, so nice ideas in training modules cannot replace effective skills that enable them to advance from poverty. For the trainees from the slums this is life and death.

Whatever training processes, they need to be designed so as to fit into a lifelong learning curve for leaders. One item that is germane to the discussion is the flexibility of schedule needed for graduate-level and adult-learning as students juggle life, family, work and study. The unpredictability of life means that shorter commitments are wiser.

Thus the MATUL is a short 39 unit degree at its core. Often theology faculty will add a number of courses,

Transformational Urban Leadership: Carving out a Vocational Training Sector

Contributing Sector 1: Theology/Missions

Cultural & Urban Economic, Anthropological, Sociological Studies

Church Growth

Urban Spirituality Contextual Theology

Contribution: Leadership is based on church formation resulting in theology/spirituality: most courses are 1/3 Theology

Sector 4: Social Work – no significant contribution, except in advocacy or distribution of goods/money to marginalized

Core

Grassroots Theology

Urban Poor Movement Leadership

Contributing Sector 2: Business Leadership Studies
Social Entrepreneurship

Small Business and Organizational Development

Community Economics

Transformational Leadership

Contribution: Poverty requires economic discipleship

Contributing Sector 3: Community Development

Community Transformation

Slum Schools, Health Programs, Advocacy Marginalized, etc.

Contribution: Once established Slum Church engage holistically

Image: Defining the domain (Vocational training sector) in relationship to contributing disciplines

but it seems wiser that if students wish to go more deeply into theology that the MATUL transitions them into an MDiv. A ladder of credible certificates or diplomas at grassroots or graduate level seems a wiser future direction, than lengthy degree Systems.

Adaptations to Learning Styles

The delivery process to be effective has to maximize engagement through a diversity of learning styles.

- Visual (spatial):You prefer using pictures, images, and spatial understanding.
- Aural (auditory-musical): You prefer using sound and music.
- Verbal (linguistic): You prefer using words, both in speech and writing.
- Physical (kinesthetic): You prefer using your body, hands and sense of touch.
- Logical (mathematical): You prefer using logic, reasoning and systems.
- Social (interpersonal): You prefer to learn in groups or with other people.
- Solitary (intrapersonal): You prefer to work alone and use self-study.[23]

In the MATUL, the linguistic or word-based learner

trained through the academic system will do well, as will the logical learner, as online design is based on logic and the program design has logical progressions. Because courses are delivered on-site at partner schools or online from APU, with weekly face to face engagement, the interpersonal is developed. Intrapersonal is significant in online learning. The kinesthetic learning style is covered through the internships and action-based learning assignments to some extent. By creating videos of each topic, the aural is accentuated. Thus the online delivery of the MATUL is well designed for maximum engagement, through the face-to-face (synchronous) or local delivery.

In other schools, each adjunct or professor needs to work with the program director to consider this diversity of learning style. I train my students to present graphically-designed assignments, as all future communication will be web-based. One student was consistently deeply upset. She was an A+ student, who was brilliant with words. She could not think in pictures. Meanwhile in that class I had six artists. They took off into realms of creativity. No professor had given them the liberty to exercise their style of learning before.

11
Grassroots Learning Networks

Pr Lukwago, Ugandan Encarnação Alliance Urban Pastors' Network Coordinator

The Idea

As more and more Christians around the globe learn about the Kingdom of God and its significance to their communities through transformational development and incarnational leadership, there have arisen many hundreds of multiplying church movements within the slums. Often these churches are led by pastors lacking in the resources and appropriate training to continue this multiplication of Kingdom principles.

With the aid of technology, it is possible to reach these pastors and leaders all around the globe. Our desire as a network is to multiply training (using existing training models where they exist or creating new ones) for these slum leaders through Grassroots Learning Networks in a manner that is easily disseminated and replicated around the world.

By building five levels of personnel and technologically relevant means of trans-

ferral, training of these leaders can occur in blocs of six week courses on key paradigms.

The central dynamic is facilitators on the ground facilitating face-to-face discussions regarding the 10 core paradigms[24] needed to move to holistic Kingdom-style ministry in the local context.

From there, leaders are taught how to teach the material themselves and go out to teach others in their community, who will also be taught to teach others.

Thus through the Grassroots Learning Networks, these multiplying movements can be provided the needed boost to continue multiplying, along with encouraging these local leaders to transmit their knowledge to the next generation of urban movement leaders to continue the work of the Kingdom in their own languages, cultures, and locales. The latter means translation is needed at the local level.

The Need

Today, there are 1.4 billion people living in the slums. Contingently, there are multiplying movements of churches throughout most of the third-world cities where these slums exist. However, they largely lack holism, and struggle without the Biblical teaching on basic economic issues which sets communities free. Additionally, there is practically no one caring for the pastors of these church movements. No one facilitates them to move from a simple gospel to the fullness of the gospel of the Kingdom that transforms all. Consequently, there is a need to provide not only emotional, spiritual, and social care to these pastors, but also biblical training on church leadership, preaching, and social action within their local contexts.

The Vision

The aim is lifelong learning by these pastors around the globe through story-based courses in order for them to understand the processes for developing urban poor people's churches using the theological framework of the Kingdom of God. This has been ongoing through the Encarnação Alliance.

Through 35 years of establishing organizations in the slums and the Encarnação Alliance that links 400 of these, there is some responsibility to forward the multiplication of effective concepts.

Take one course as an example. During 20 years of setting up story-telling training for semi-literate grassroots slum movement leaders in scores of cities, ten principles of a Theology of Cooperative Economics have been crystallized into economic transformation for slum churches, radically shifting their economic conditions. The establishing of the MATUL includes delivery of a graduate level course on Community Economics which integrates these into academia, and enables the training of movement leadership ready to multiply these ideas at the grassroots.

In Uganda, Pr J. B Lukwago has, over ten years, taught these concepts to leaders of 168 churches, resulting in many attempts at economic development and transformation of the role of pastor and flock, as the pastor seeks to serve the flock to become self-sufficient financially.

The Strategy

Encarnação Alliance

The vision of the Alliance is to see churches established that proclaim the Good News of the Kingdom of God among the slum dwellers of the world's poorest cities and model true Christian living on the example of Jesus Christ.

Macro goals:
- To train urban poor church planters
- To train urban poor community development

workers
- To network city leaders
- To develop a Kingdom perspective in God's servants

The Network

Currently, we are linked to about 400 slum movements. There have been learning networks in 20 cities, with some still extant. Meanwhile, with the MA in Transformational Urban Leadership, we are graduating around 50 students a year in 8 cities on 5 continents who are eager to train others around the globe.

.

Flipped Learning

Our goal is to provide the training content through a server and to have the discussions face-to-face within each city. The internet is used mainly for delivering the curriculum while the small groups are for spiritual formation, as iron sharpens iron.

Grapevine Model

Each student or a small group is considered a "grape" as they learn together. Each cluster of grapes is a region, distinguished by a unique language and culture. The standardized training (the good juice) flows along the internet to the clusters and then to the individual grapes.

The Knack of Non-complex Delivery

We focus on integrating materials that can be easily disseminated via mobile phones and tablets. Every pastor and business in the slums has one. The website is designed first for mobile devices, using responsive design frameworks such as Bootstrap.

Delivery

Only four formats work well across a wide range of platforms, on low-bandwidths, and are familiar to all end-users. They are: MP3 audio, PDF, doc and html. We utilize these formats for our material so that all will be able to access the files.

Video

Currently, there is no common format across devices for video. Format Factory, however, can be used to provide consistency. Due to this, we will primarily rely on audio files with occasional videos. As an alternative, it is possible to use narrated Power Points, which are also much more manageable in regard to file size.

The Knack of Packaging

MAF-LT has done a great deal of work in finding offline methods of delivering training and has developed two key apps: Lumin and Estante = Bookshelf in Span-

Grassroots Workers' Training: Chennai

ish is available through Richard Morris at rmorris@maflt.org.

Solid, Reliable Server

One of the better alternatives is a hosted server in a co-location facility. This costs $100 per month for 100mbps bandwidth, and the server hardware is included. This can handle thousands of simultaneous users for web pages and streaming audio, but would slow down considerably if a lot of HD videos were being streamed. Since most students are not online all at the same time, one server could handle 50,000 students on mobile devices. This seems like the most plausible option. Additionally, we can use the Lumin app for mobile phones, which is the equivalent of Moodle for cell phones.

Knowledge Levels.

From my consultations with urban poor workers over the decades, I have identified 19 paradigm shifts needed for urban poor workers, to move to effective holistic church-planting. However, there is a range of levels of delivery.

Thus there are two delivery systems, two different styles:. Complex master's and mass-produced grass-root to large numbers of a simple product. A master's reaches a few with a complex product.

Prototypes Needed

Currently, we have identified that six week courses work most effectively. As an additional requirement, the trainees will be required to study for 6 hours outside of the course. With only three hours per week available to most busy lay people in ministry, time is limited. Additionally, we have observed that any course longer than six weeks seems to result in high drop-out rates, especially for those done online.

Personnel

The Nodes - Key to Multiplication

Our vision is to see multiplication happening through cohorts of from 10-25 individuals who will then train perhaps 15 more, who train 15 more, etc. resulting in 15 x 15 x 15 x 15 x 15 x 15 individuals trained. The key to this multiplication lies in the facilitators and the leaders of these urban poor learning networks within each city. These facilitators need proper training, as described below, with the use of cell phones or tablets. Additionally, there is an emphasis on a commitment to an ethos, and a value system.

Committee Planners & Writers

Some of these modules exist through partnering organizations and can be upgraded to a common standard.

The planners and writers of new modules need to be selected and invited to join this project during conferences/consultations of urban pastors and leaders from around the globe. These planners and writers are the main source of the material and its dissemination to the city coordinators, facilitators, trainers, and trainees. They revise and update the material as needed and serve as a sort of board for future developments. We have not found the learning network coordinators to be skilled at this level of materials design. They are skilled in working with their people and delivering training.

City coordinators need to be selected for each city in which the training will take place. Their primary role is as a resource to the facilitators in regard to training and problem management as well as a connection to the committee.

Learning Network Facilitators

Facilitators are the primary educators for this program. Through them, AND if we have materials they can use, we can educate the first group of trainers to then go and form cohorts of 15-25 to train others. As technology is relatively straightforward for delivery of the teaching material, the greatest challenge is finding, training and sustaining effective facilitators to conduct the learning. The key to tracking volunteer facilitators and keeping them "on track" is utilizing a web-based project management system on a server, such as 2Plan. Not only will this be helpful for the facilitators, but it will also provide information and data on how the project is running.

Trainers

Each facilitator is toseek out 15-25 individuals within their community to train through the learning material. These trainers will then be trained on how to teach the material to others within their community and social spheres. Once they have completed the courses, then they will find 15 individuals of their own to train.

Trainees

These are the final recipients of the learning material. Having been trained by the trainers, they will also go out into their communities to find 15 more individuals to train and spread the knowledge.

Technical Requirements

Our attempts to use cell-phone delivery have not proven effective - *at this time*. Smart phones are required, and they are expensive and the cost of downloading is expensive. Nevertheless, we should develop everything in responsive modes.Given that the trainers have computer access, then the need is to provide computer cafes that also become training centres. John Edmiston has identified the requirements for setting these up.[25]

In the next section we will explore one grassroots example in India, then expand reflections on technology in Global Learning Networks.

Some Partner Schools

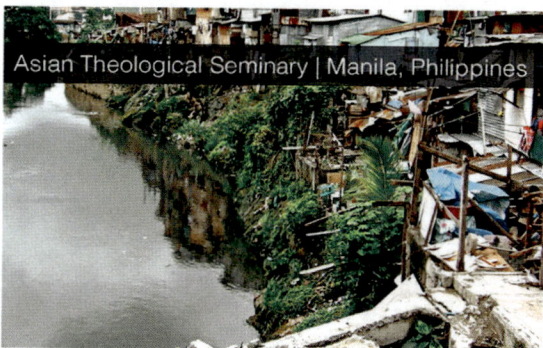

Church-Based Grassroots Training for Evangelization in India

By *Hruda Ranjan Lohora, Academic Dean, Mission India Theological Seminary.*

The Context

India is a pluralistic nation in which around 1.35 billion people[26] live with a tangible constitution of secularism, democracy, and equality. It has 30 states and 7 union territories. Among 1.35 billions of population in India, around 70 % of populations live in villages (Rural) and the other 30 % live in the cities (Urban). Among the 70 % of the rural population, around 68 % are literate (Know reading & writing) and 32 % are illiterate. Among 30 % of urban population, around 84 % are literate and other 16 % are illiterate. Among the states and union territories, some of them are having higher literacy rate up to 94 % of their population (Kerala, Lakshadweep, Mizoram, etc.) and some of them have lower illiteracy rate between 62 and 66 % of their population (Bihar, Arunachal Pradesh, Jharkhand, etc). [27]

As per the survey of World Bank in 2013, India has the highest number of people living in below poverty line. It accounts for one in three of the poor population worldwide with the largest number of people living under the international USD 1.90 a day poverty line, more than 2.50 times as many as the 86 million in Nigeria, which has the second largest population of the poor worldwide.[28] Perhaps, this could have checked if the increase rate of unemployment in India had halted and backwardness of the people are advanced and uplifted. There are around 31 million Indians are jobless as per the data released by Times of India groups on March 6, 2018.[29] While the literacy rate increases in India so also the unemployment rate as the Government is unable create new jobs for the educated youth as compare to the educational growth. The Dalit community, which are officially known as scheduled castes (20 %) and scheduled tribes (9 %) are occupying around 29 % of India's population. Be-

sides, there are 41 % of backward class living in India. It means around 70 % of India's population are to be given serious attention for their upliftment socially, economically and educationally.

About one in six Indian city residents lives in an urban slum with unsanitary conditions, which are unfit for human habitation. The census report of 2011 identified 13.8 million households, about 64 million people located in the city slums nationwide. That is 17.40 percent of all urban households, which account for roughly one third of India's 1.2 population of 2011. More than 40 percent of households in Mumbai, Indian's financial capital and largest city with 19 million people, are located in overcrowded shantytowns where most residents are squatting illegally and many have little access to basic sanitation.[30] Such stories are found in every city of India.

Throughout its long history, the Hindu tradition that occupies 79.80 % of the population has shared a common soil with other religious groups. India is the homeland of Buddhist tradition with 0.70 % of the population, which flourished in India from the time of the Buddha in the sixth century BCE and expanded to other parts of the world becoming national religion of few of them. The Jain tradition of monks, nuns, and laity, which is the contemporary of the Buddhist tradition, occupies 0.40 % of the population in India.

The Christian tradition with 2.30 % of the population, also has ancient roots in India, where Christians trace their origins back to the Apostle Thomas in the first century. Other religions that include the Jewish tradition, which has an old community started by traders in the southern state of Kerala and in Bombay and the Zoroastrian tradition with roots in what is now Iran occupy 0.70 % of the population. Beginning in the eleventh century, the Muslim tradition took root in India and developed a distinctive Indo-Muslim culture occupying 14.20 % of the population. Finally, the Sikh tradition began in northwest India in the sixteenth century with the teaching of Guru Nanak and has evolved into a vibrant and distinctive religious community occupying 1.70 % of the population. With the arrival of British in India through the establishment of East India Company in the late seventeenth century, came Protestant Christianity and the mission movement. While the trade between India and the West began to develop, the flows of intellectual and religious thought traveled back and forth as well.[31].

What is Grassroots Training?

Grassroots training may be defined as an "Elementary preparation of the lay-Christians with a basic skill of presenting the Gospel in a given situation." The lay-Christians may be either from urban or rural, literate or illiterate, but must be from the community for the community.[32].

The basic assumption that every member at any local church can be an Evangelist. The only necessary thing she/he does not know as to how to do the job of evangelism. In the present dispensation, the church has reduced the 'ministry' of evangelism to either a 'paid staff' or the 'gifted person' or the seminary trained 'missionary'. All these are a myth the fact is that every person is and can do the job of an evangelist, they just need to know how to.[33] It conveys the philosophy of church-based education, which takes the education to the local churches to be trained in their context instead of bringing them to a seminary or a school. Training at their context, at their level and by a person who has done this and NOT by a person who has the theory but not practices the implementation of the teaching. These training ought to be as non-formal as possible because people are not used to the formal seminary type education in the local church set-up. The basics could include as simple as possible. Just why, what and how of evangelism to how to study the Bible and how to communicate the message of the Bible (preach/teach).

The lessons on the fundamentals of Christian Life and Christian calling to be included emphasizing the cost and demands of following Christ and the Christian life. This is where people will learn the privilege of sufferings (Phil. 1:29; I Pet. 1:6 ff.). The training must include lessons on "Justice and advocacy" so that at times of attack and persecution they know what to do and where to turn to. Keeping mind the cultural sensibility and economic sustainability, the training must include the lessons on social entrepreneurship.

It has been well researched that Grassroots level training is not only sustainable but they are also growing. Prof. Hebert Hoefer's book, *Churchless Christianity* came out of his Ph.D. dissertation bears the testimony that local Christians in and around Chennai city, mostly Dalits, have been living witnesses of the reality of Christ which they have experienced in their lives and now have grown from the first generation to the second.[34] The research among the Dalits and Scheduled Castes in the Eastern Uttar Pradesh and Western Bihar are yet another testimony that they have grown from 10,000 local churches in the 1980's to well over 23,000 in between 2006-2008. A number of believers

have more than doubled during the same period.[35]

Who are the Grassroots Workers?

Grass-roots level workers are the local evangelists who are involved in reaching their own people with the Gospel. The traditional belief that grass-roots level workers are only the tribal evangelists was found to be wrong as there are such workers found in rural and urban as well must be trained and sent in large numbers to reach the urban, rural and tribal in India.[36].

Therefore, Dr. K. Rajendran[37] writes that the grassroots workers are the normal Christians, who are instrumental to build each other in Christian maturity. They may or may not be theologically trained priests. They may or may not be the poor, the downtrodden or the lowliest of the society. The grassroots workers can be either from the rural or the urban areas. They are not based on the income and expenditures brackets, not based on the "haves" and "the have-nots."[38].

Another way, the grassroots workers are lay-Christians both from the poor and the rich, who are in contact with the society. They are mostly from the theologically untrained background. These are the grassroots, which need to be taught in order that they will penetrate their own friends by their words and deeds that Christ has changed their lives and has the power to change their struggling colleagues as well. Thus, they will play the role as the lighters or illuminators of the society transforming them from the worldliness to the Christ-likeness.

Many sense the potential of the laymen in E-1 and E2 evangelism and in some cases E3 evangelism.[39]

Rev. Imotemjen Air, the General Secretary of the Council of Baptist Churches of North East India (CBC-NEI), in emphasizing the way to mobilize the laity whom he described as the powerful agents, wrote:

> The Task of evangelization rests on both the people of the pew and the people of the pulpit.... Laymen and women are the spearheads of the church's mission to the world. The lay people have an advantage [to] witness in families, shops, labor unions, political centers, social clubs, and etc.[40].

Indigenous Grassroots Training by Mission India

In 1996, Mission India (MI) has emerged out of a vision "To equip young men and women to become

Christ-like leaders for grassroots evangelism & Church planting in the unreached villages and cities of India & beyond." At present, it has 28 Bible Schools in different parts of India including one in Myanmar and one in Nepal that offers Grassroots Training in regional languages. Among these, Mission India Theological Seminary (MITS) offers various programs like Grassroots training in regional language and Diploma to Masters in the English language. MI has various other projects as well, like evangelism & Church planting, Children homes, Summer Bible Schools, Secular Schools, Hospital/Medical clinics, vocational training, micro-finance, humanitarian, etc.

Until March 2018, Mission India Bible Schools & Mission India Theological Seminary have trained and sent out almost 6500 lay-leaders with grassroots training for grassroots evangelism and Church planting. Out of 6500 trained lay-leaders, 400 are still working with Mission India Trinity Churches and converted almost 25,000 people to Christ in the context of antagonism and violence.[41]

Mission India Grassroots training are campus and curriculum-based formal education in the regional languages. It takes seriously the three domains of learning in order that the trainees can be trained holistically by imparting knowledge, developing character, and instilling ministerial skills. During this training period, they are expected to use the library, participate in the extracurricular activities of the Seminary, and the weekend evangelistic tour for evangelism and Church planting. The courses offered to them are common to the curricula that most Bible Colleges and Seminaries offer. Nevertheless, the indigenous grassroots training becomes a backbone of the local churches for the whole church's involvement in God's Mission

Why Church-based Grassroots Training for the Lay Christians?

"One research proves that 87% of our theological graduates want to work only among the 30% of the population who live in the rural areas (1979-1999)."[42] As per the census of India in 2011, 68.84 % of the total population live in rural areas.[43] Realistically, most of the theological graduates in India look for the ministry opportunities in the Bible Colleges as instructors, in well-established Churches as pastors/associate-pastors/deacons, in reputed organizations as directors/coordinators/administrators, in well-established children's homes as managers/wardens, and etc. Moreover, most of them like to be in the cities or developed towns, not in the rural areas. Perhaps, only

23 % of them go to the mission field as grassroots level workers for grassroots evangelism and Church planting. Not more than 1% of the Christian populations in India go for a theological training, and among which majority of them are found in the grassroots ministries. Keeping in view of the original concept of grassroots training, the entire believers must be focused.

In 2013, the Church-based missiological education incorporated with courses of transformational urban leadership was introduced at Nagpur Diocese of Church of North India by Dr. Hruda Ranjan Lohora and Rt. Rev. Paul Dupare in focus of urban poor transformation. 25 lay-leaders were graduated and all of them are serving in their local churches in various ways. Today, there are 12 lay-leaders under training at Mahila Sadan of All Saints Cathedral Compound (www.myindiamission.org).

In 2017, Mission India has introduced a Church-Based Theological Training (CBTT) under the leadership of Dr. Saji Lukos and is coordinated by Rev. Satish Sukhadeve. Today, CBTT is functioning in 14 different churches where 450 believers are being given training for grassroots evangelism and church planting. After its initiation, 57 believers, who have successfully completed the training, were given graduation. The courses offered in CBTT are quite similar to that of Mission India Bible Colleges except for a couple of courses on transformational leadership. The graduates are being the active members of the local churches rendering their service for the mission of God inside and outside the Church.[44]

Analysis and Suggestions

The outcomes of the grassroots training signals the vital need of such training in India. However, seeing every corner of the Indian context, a church-based training is highly recommended so as to cover everyone in the local churches both poor and rich, literacy and illiteracy, physically challenged and healthy, and socially weak and strong in the community.

Mission India has a vision for Grassroots evangelism and Church planting, which is a positive side to have a specific vision for a specific task. It offers grassroots trainings in the local languages so as to develop local Church planters for their community. However, there requires more mission practitioners to be used as trainers, who can simplify the courses in the level of grassroots trainees' understanding than theologically trained educators, who can be more theological and theoretical in course delivery. It focuses the literary

population whereas around 16 % of urban population and 32 % of rural population are illiterates, and thereby, a step to be taken for the inclusion of non-formal and informal system of training so as to find the illiterate lay-Christians in the club. Besides, an experienced-based learning is to be employed allocating more times in the activities and less times in the classrooms.

*G*rassroots Training in India for Indians

Since Grassroots training is meant for the lay-Christians, the courses to be designed as per the local context and the learning capacity of the learners. As to my understanding of doing mission in the context, the courses given below would be quite appropriate.

1. Indian Religiosity & Cultural Identity
2. Indian Constitution & Fundamental Rights
3. The lifestyle of the people: Urban and Rural Comparisons
4. God and the People in the Bible: Bible Survey
5. Biblical Principles for Community Transformation
6. Educational Ministries in the localities
7. Story Telling & Dialogical Methods of Communication.
8. Cultivating Christ-like Character: Four Gospels
9. Primary Health Care & Basic Counseling Methods
10. Principles of Church Planting & Church Growth (Acts)
11. Social Entrepreneurship & Transformational Leadership
12. Advocacy and Land Rights

As stated in paragraphs 3 and 4, around 70 % of India's population, who live in poverty level to be given a special care and attention. It is possible only through reaching them with a remedial measure needed in accordance the situation they are in. The courses I have suggested above, emanated out of my personal experience and observation for several years as a slum dweller and a trainer of transformational urban leadership bearing in mind the poverty stricken community in the slums. To my view, this set of courses for Grassroots training would be fitting rightly for the transformation of the community economically, socially, and educationally. I trust that the Grassroots training in transformational urban leadership for the lay-Christians living in and working closely with poor community in urban slums, will produce a positive impact on the slum community living in slums in both urban and rural sectors.

MATUL student Grecia Reyes, implements the MATUL theology of "hanging out" in New Delhi

12

Innovative Technology in Urban Missiological Education

It's 11 p.m. my time, 5 a.m. in Mozambique, and in Manila, Bangkok, Chennai, and Nairobi times in between. The eight inset videos of students on my screen are dynamic, though periodically one disappears in Nairobi, due to low bandwidth. Others turn off their video to conserve their power on their modems, but remain engaged. Maybe one is sleeping.

The discussion is poignant – about land ownership. In the scriptures and in their communities! Poignant with story! Poignant with commitment! Poignant with character formation! Poignant with a depth of new dimensions of theology!.

"I grew up in a missionary family, so we have never owned a home", shares one, currently living in a slum home in a tough Indian city. "As I read Brueggemann, I realized that I am committed to a lifetime following the Lord with no place to lay my head!" There was a quietness in the presence of God across cyberspace at a moment of such commitment.

In a cohort that has spent 18 months together online 1,2,3 times a week, there was only affirmation that this too was within the mandate of the scriptures we were discussing. The experienced missionary from Mozambique affirmed them both in prayer.

Character! Cohort relationships! Spiritual formation! Pastoral Care! Engagement with reality! Best practice urban missions education!!! What are some of the elements that underlie the educational philosophy and dynamics of such a delivery system!?

Disruptive Innovations

Disruptive innovations build on the existing infrastructure and paradigms within an industry. The new innovations, and products begin at the edges and are often in the least productive areas of those industries, so are not an early threat.

The first disruptive paradigm I brought to missions was that of *incarnational mission in the slums* in the late 1970's and 1980's as I lived among the poor, publishing *Companion to the Poor*, which disseminated the ideas through the major missions. Now many hundreds of cross-cultural workers have followed those ideas.

The second was of *incarnational Protestant apostolic orders* among the urban poor - a crossover from the Franciscan preaching friars. The innovation was outworked in the structures of *Servants to Asia's Urban Poor, Servant-Patners* and others followed.

The third was of a *master's' degree as the locus of integrating the knowledge globally* needed for the training of urban poor workers. This was outworked in the MATUL in five universities.

The next phase of innovation is multiplying the domainthrough *grassroots learning networks.*

Five Phases in Urban Missiological Delivery

To explore scaling of the latter, technological advances are significant. The following is a replay of the technological style of

The Innovative and Structural Characteristics of the Pentecostal Spirit.

We began with the Spirit of creation, the innovator in Part 1. We have explored his nature in wisdom education in Part 2 and 3. In Part 4 we are examining his ways in creating structure. Including the structure of the internet in delivery of an action-reflection-style education.

missions training over the last hundred years.

Phase 1: (1920'2-1970's) Missionaries were trained in Seminaries or Bible Schools that focused on knowledge and character formation prior to being sent to the field. During the first two years of cross-cultural adaptation, they were then mentored on the field by older missions team leaders.

The next phases sought to deliver the training to workers on site in-field. The principle was *do not disturb the context or means of production.*

Phase 2 (1970's): TEE was an early form of dissemination. Theological Education by Extension used the mail system, and sent out written workbooks, and used mail to send back quizzes for evaluation.

Phase 3 (1980's): Fuller Theological Seminary then pioneered master's level missions education, that was reproduced at other missions schools.

- **Content:** A "banking system" of knowledge. The professor is expert. His expertise lies in readings. He downloads knowledge into the heads of students.
- **Delivery System:** using audio cassettes of professors in classes, and books posted out to missionaries around the world.
- Lectures had been taped. Lectures and Readings were typed up.

Praxis-Based Education: On the job, incarnational, cohort, weekly online, internship, language mastery, internships, mentoring - all lead to quality outcomes.

- **Evaluation:** Assignments consisted of two major papers and some book reviews. Human interaction was minimal.
- **Retention:** very low

Phase 4 (late 1990's - 2009): This morphed into *asynchronous* online education (that is, content is delivered online without classroom contact, but with occasional discussions with a human Facilitator. Everything is based on paperwork). It continued the traditions. However, faculty were not impressed at the mass multiplication and depersonalization of education.

- **Content:** This was still following the "banking system" of knowledge. The professor is expert. His expertise lies in readings. He downloads knowledge into the heads of students.
- **Delivery system:** audio tapes now moved to video recordings of professors teaching and quoting from their written materials. Human interaction now included some video calls for professor – student interaction, but essentially the system was based on a knowledge transfer, not a group learning process, driven by student experiences.
- **Retention** is low.
- **Evaluation:** Without the human communication there was minimal character formation and little leadership formation, just knowledge of theories. Clearly, with such a process there could also be minimal pastoral care.

This phase began to highlight some major problems with online learning. First, the problem of *transactional distance*, as this form of impersonal asynchronous online education creates relational distance and hence considerable retention issues, . Many ways around this are suggested, such as *Empathetic Pedagogy*. I was just informed by one expert how to make brief personal videos, the need to occasionally chat with students, a weekly welcome communiqué, where a 3-minute video would add to the humanity. But at best these are fixes. A typical statement:.

> *Many people have the misconception that online learning is nothing more than a virtual vending machine where students serve themselves with little or no interaction with instructors. This dehumanizing of online learning has consequences. Online students drop out at a higher rate than their face-to-face counterparts. Those who remain are less satisfied than students in traditional classes, and large numbers develop feelings of isolation and discouragement* (McCombs & Vakili, 2005; Montazemi, 2006; Passerini, 2007; Summers, Waigandt, & Whittaker, 2005).[45]

Phase 5 (2010-18): When the MATUL began, we pioneered a new style, not because we set out to do so, simply because we had developed within a different educational philosophy as urban educators. I had always been up to speed with technology and didn't know any better. I was unaware that you should not do face to face education online.

Concept of Education: Education is not a "banking system of downloadable knowledge", it is a professor's facilitation that unpacks the knowledge existent in the student's engagement in action with the local culture and context (Friere).

Content definition is initially derived from student engagement in the local context through action-reflection processes and internships. This they then interface with the local or global literature in reflection that is delivered to classmates. The professor (as facilitator) integrates this with the major literature in each field (as expert). The professors needs skill to determine a pathway of experiences step by step and to identify readings that enable reflection so that the student master's the breadth of theory and praxis in each field. (This is messy. Be warned!! The professor will never get high ratings because the evaluation systems used on the academy are based on the banking model, with the professor being the expert and every detail of the course being defined on paper, up-front).

This is largely **inductive education,** but some content by its nature is **didactic,** so an ebb and flow from student to professor-driven learning is normative in each class. An extreme pedagogical mindset is not realistic.

Primary delivery system: Face to face online. SKYPE had become viable globally by 2010. In the cities (not rural) up to 2014, mostly online discussion was viable with up to five nodes. We then used VSee, which accommodated lower bandwidth better and up to 9 cities. By 2017, Zoom was now available. Cables were laid to East Africa, so now clarity of face-to-face communication is very good up to 8 or so nodes (with up to 4 students in a city on each one). We have not experimented with more globally.

Evaluating Personal Transformation

Inherent in a Freirean or a Constructivist approach to education is a goal of transformation; both of the person, the community of learners and the contextual realities. This does not fit well with standards-based testing common in the US, which can manifest the extremes of another educational philosophy, that of Behaviourism growing from B. F, Skinner and the famous Pavlov dogs. A less extreme, limited or modified use of standards however is not incompatible with a constructivist approach.

The more complex evaluation within our urban missions training has to do not with evaluating transfer of knowledge but transmission of character and values. There are five areas of missions training related to these that are crucial.

1. **Skills and Knowledge** can both be measured by papers that integrate local, global knowledge with experiences or reports of internships Missions Education is centred on spiritual formation, cross-cultural capacities and leadership formation as students cross the cultural divides (Illich, 1957). Each course identifies some character or spiritual formation objectives, but these tend to be diverse according to students backgrounds and experiences, so are more difficult to quantify than knowledge content objectives. (IDEA, the common US methodology for measuring professor effectiveness, measures faith integration, but does not measure educating for spiritual formation).

2. **Cross-cultural capacities** are well documented in missions circles but very different to intercultural cultural capacities required for example by nurses in the US. The World Evangelical Alliance Training Commission for many years developed analyses of these. The foundational framework and research underlying the MATUL were derived from their work.

3. **Survival capacities.** Those values, skills, attitudes and habits that enable longevity on the field are better defined from work by the Missionary Care networks (Hay, Rob, Valerie Lim, Detlef Bloecher, & Sarah Hay, 2007).

4. **Leadership Formation.** Leadership education can be through didactic downloads (banking model) or actual education using inductive methods based on action-reflection models. Leadership education is multidimensional. Leadership trait formation can be defined. Specific elements of leadership experiences can be developed that cover some skills, some relational dynamics such as team building, some leadership within organisational analysis exercises. (These can be measured through internship reports, and papers).

5. **Pastoral Care and Reentry:** Spiritual formation can be utilized as a basis of self-care. But the complex experiences on the field are better handled by a pastoral care approach. This requires someone locally who can monitor situations, and a backup skilled pastoral care person. Since formal counselling is forbidden by the American Psychological Association cross-culturally, a trained chaplain is preferred. Defining the dynamic of such relationships is important but also requires tailoring to the skills of the personnel. Training of a chaplain is needed.

The above goals requires significant **human interaction** between professor and students. Guidance across the degree as to what learning experiences and partnerships with local organizations is crucial.

Formation of learning communities. Deep levels of loving, supportive community develop in each cohort. This diffuses the pastoral care and learning support to a significant extent, and is a significant part of the character formation process. Anecdotal evidence from students ranks this very highly.

Measurement: How do we measure the development and growth of these cultural or character or style capacities across the degree? This is a lot more fuzzy than behaviourism can cope with. They are evident to both professor and other students, and evident to supervisors in internships. We can measure impact on local communities, and anecdotal reports from internship supervisors and local church supervisors. Reports on actions can demonstrate skills and leadership. This issue will be reflected on in greater depth in Book 3 as each course is analyzed, for example the use of Psychological testing in Urban Spirituality, of Cross-Cultural skills analysis, and individual discussion of progressions in dealing with pain, trauma and grief.

Synchronous Face to Face Online Learning

Students must engage with their context, the course material, with their peers and with their instructor. In synchronous engagement weekly there is more communication than in a face to face class on campus. It is in fact intense, very personal. There are personalities! The precise detailed story teller who takes ten minutes for each story, the quick thinker who has an immediate answer, the hesitant Hispanic, careful with words who has to be drawn out, the late coming philosopher, arriving 30 minutes into each class – it's the normal chaos of group engagement.

And the role of the professor becomes paramount – humility is critical. When there is criticism, humbly receiving it – such as when a date is incorrect (which in online systems is not infrequent), when there is disagreement about an issue, listening to the various sides and adjudicating wisely, the skill of integrating a lesson and bringing it to high point of motivation based on the discoveries, adding in expertise, connecting the dots, so all leave with a renewed sense of energy. Facial expressions from eight countries - some bored, some arrogant, some enthusiastic - mean the professor constantly is reeling them in to engagement, pressing them forward to commitments, stirring up their curiosity and imagination.

In contrast, as I listen to a training video on the traditional asynchronous learning of the 1990's still in vogue in higher education IT, it states: *The weakest link in online learning is engagement with the instructor. Online instructors are often perceived as absent or apathetic or both"* I find myself bewildered!! Why would they use such a backwards technological approach from a decade ago, when the technology has moved on from asynchronous forums and paperwork, to interactive video cohorts working together across cohorts?!

Retention

Our MATUL international retention rates have been 78-83% for students over 2-3 years of study. A training video tells us, *Online students drop out at a higher rate than their face-to-face counterparts.* This is backed up by statistics elsewhere from the department of education: Of the top ten universities the retention rate averages: First year full time 55%, First year part time 39%.[46].

The training video goes on to say, *Feelings of isolation is the number one reason for dropping out!!!* Our students hang out online. Even if they have to travel for two hours to a class they travel, because there is a supportive environment. There is no isolation!

Mentored courses

That has implications. Content is not the most important felt need, relationships are! So often we deviate to deal with a particular pastoral care issue as a group – the pain of engaging with destitution, the frustration as they work with an organization and realize there is corruption, the despair as they fail day after day in language learning. They don't always want more knowledge, they want support. And in that is the learning. Knowledge is not written, redacted, philosophical constructs.

So we extend Freire to online delivery. Knowledge is warm, human, relational, wrapped up in a loving community of peers. The humanity is in the unpacking of the contextual realities. And the emotive responses to those realities of oppression, dispossession, poverty, dysfunction. We are not equipping students to publish papers (Well we do, but that is not the primary goal). We are equipping them to engage, to feel, to reflect, to interpret, to act. **Building a cohort community of peers** is critical in this. A Freirean approach works with communal discussion.

.

Knowledge then is not impersonal. It is human. In reflection we link it back to theories and behind them to philosophies. Our students complete a degree well able to converse with diverse fields that impinge on poverty. But at its core it is not impersonal constructs of ideas. It cannot be roboticized.

Transactional Distance

Our aim in a master's-level program is not thousands but mentoring 15-20 (15 has been demonstrated as an optimal learning size; 20 is a viable financial number) or maximum of 30 at a time. In grassroots learning the aim is different, multiplication to thousands. But that also can best be done with local Learning Network Trainers who deal with the relational aspects.

Thus, why not utilize face-to-face zoom technology we use to communicate as the primary vehicle? That seems essential for Masters level training. It is essential for training of trainers at the grassroots. For at the grassroots we cannot utilize mass multiplication of the internet. The trainers take the materials and multiply them. And they are the ones where transmission of character and values become central. This incidentally is good risk management strategy also -it increases retention, and decreases human struggles.

Having explored technology, we progress in the next chapter to consider the differences infrastructure between grassroots certificate and diploma level training with the upper levels of training. But first, a case study in an alternative technological delivery system. One that has not demonstrated a way forward, but it is of value to explore why not as it indicates the current limits of technology!

MATUL Commission, Manila, 2015 in King Solomon Learning Centre in Tatalon, an upgraded slum area. The Commission has been the source of much innovation.

You never change things by fighting the existing reality.

To change things build a new model that makes the existing model obsolete.

—Buckminster Fuller

CASE STUDY in INNOVATION:

EXPERIMENTAL DESIGN OF CELL-BASED DELIVERY OF MATUL CONTENT TO SLUM PASTORS

Background

The MATUL has been an incubator of creative learning processes. (1) Its foundation has been to train slum movement leaders in their context of learning, or move them into residency is the slums. Whoever heard of a masters degree for thinking poor people? (2) Its methodology has included synchronous online delivery (3) to 8 cities. (4) It has multiplied a new urban theology methodology called Transformational Conversations. (5) Most classes are action-reflection beginning with the stories of the week. It has resulted in (6) the development of social entrepreneurs (7) uniquely trained in a theology from among the poor, (8) and in skills sets in all the major aspects of urban poor ministry. (9) The research project and other courses result in action such as forming schools in slums; funding $1.2 million for toilets in Kibera, Nairobi, so girls can go to high school; expanding HIV/AIDS programs; designing a program for aged-out orphans to adapt to life…

Design of Next Innovation

This sense of multiplication of training needed further development and lead to innovation within the MATUL. The plan was for students to package materials from Masters training into oral learner content level for slum workers in the partner Slum Learning Networks. They needed to design a reproducible system as part of the degree. This included a new cell- phone accessibility that enables Network Leaders to supplement face-to-face training (computer downloaded PowerPoint or paper) with 30 days downloading mp3's to cell-phones.

By the end of this project, implementation of at least one model in reproduction of the course on Community Economics via cell phone delivery to a Grassroots Learning Network was to be accomplished.

Desired Outputs

1.   A simple reproducible model for students: to model a simple pattern of delivery of content from one of the MATUL Courses to existing slum Learning Networks of grassroots workers. This is a model that our students, graduates at APU and students and 60 faculty in 7 partner institutions should find to be easily reproducible for other courses. Result: Model Developed
2.   Immediate delivery: training to 20-30 oral learning leaders in one Slum Leaders Learning Network. Result: Done with two networks.
3.   Trainer of Trainers (Network Leaders) website, manual in a Moodle course style. Result: Half Done.
4.   Systems set up of program design processes, server and delivery of materials to multiple sites. Result: Done.

Creativity and Innovation

1.   Systematic use of new cellphone availability: Interfacing MA level training of well educated movement leaders with oral learning urban poor society is a trick in the MATUL for which we are constantly seeking innovative approaches. The creative results of past student attempts has also highlighted the need for an initial system they can

use with local leaders quickly and easily so as to get started.

2.   The disruptive innovation (Sears 2015) currently occurring in education is the explosion of 100 billion cell phones. These have now reached to every slum worker. Every pastor has a cell phone to his ear. With the network leaders having access to computers where they can download materials (notes, videos), these can be used in initial and final face-to-face days of training. In between cellphone delivery of audio mp3's is within the cost and bandwidth capacity of the workers and pastors.

Outcomes: *Delivery of Product*

1.   *Catastrophes:* One coordinator in Manila fell off a mountain breaking back and foot. In Uganda, products produced from the training were sent to an area to be sold .Intertribal warfare caused them all to be lost.

2.   *Content Development:* 30 podcasts were developed using GarageBand, and are available on a website http://www.economicdisciple.org, and downloadable to cell phones. Along with the podcasts are one-page summaries and a Bible Study series (this was a great hit) developed by various students, that the pastors can use with their people. Some extra podcasts at higher level of thinking about national economics yet to be added - not essential to most.

3.   Trainers in two cities set up an initial training, in which I was involved in English and they attempted to *translate,* then they sent the podcasts via cellphone.

4.   *Translation:* Ultimate bottleneck. No-one felt adequate to be a translator in Manila. Because we were not paying professional translators, we then had 40 participants, each translating a session, but when the local coordinator broke his foot and back, all progress has stopped. How do we get it accurate is their biggest worry? vs how do we add in local stories, proverbs, and style. Conclusion: Translation is best done through face to face SKYPE delivery which is translated on the spot and recorded at that time, then documented. Delivery in Uganda ended up as Synchronous VSee based video dialogue, when the internet worked –30% of the time. They preferred this direct dialogue as a means of converting the materials.

5.   *The network leaders* from several cities joined together in four trainer of trainers calls. The website is being modified from that. Not complete.

6.   *Evaluations* were to be made online by the students as part of the process of receiving their certificates, but these catastrophes prevented this. The design has been modified step by step as feedback came in step by step.

7.   *Technical Conclusions:* Website was laid out then redone using Square Space. The reason being one of bandwidth. We discovered that the original style sheets involve a lot of reconnecting to our US server, whereas Square Space has servers globally. But at the end of the day it is an expensive solution, as we end up paying monthly fees for each course. A further version w dveloped by the son of our Ugandan coordinator in Dreamweaver, with much greater flexibility

8.   *Local Variations in Technological Capacity:* In Uganda, as international internet connections are not good, and 80% of pastors don't have smart phones face to face delivery currently works, but some are ready for podcasts. By contrast, face to face + web- based + cellphone works in Manila – though only half the pastors have smart phones. The technology works in Bangkok, but translation needs to be done in a face-to-face context, then recorded.

Outcomes: *Sustainability Beyond the Project*

Network leaders: In 2015, the MATUL Training Commission identified a progression of courses and professors to develop this out to 16 courses. But they have been waiting for a good template, and structure, before launching. Thus, this catalyses a dozen reflective-practitioner professors globally into reproducing their expertise. The next step beyond this is to work with them to multiply the style.

Intermediate Outcomes: Three network leaders have been involved in designing delivery. The trainer of trainers site is set to be a wider hub. But the trainees do not have smart phones and every minute costs, so access to podcasts has not proven viable until the internet is expanded and becomes accessible financially to common people.

13

Vertically Integrated Delivery of Urban Poor Missiology

Our defined goal in this study is the development and delivery of a sustainable discipline of urban poor missiology. The MA in Transformational Urban Leadership becomes the centre of such a discipline. But that is only one phase.

Our mandate from the Bangkok Encarnação Alliance gathering of 2004 has been to train 50,000 leaders in holistic church-based missional work in the slums. This requires sustainable infrastructure support. Beyond the experiments and theoretical frameworks documented in this study, our desired future is vertically-integrated educational infrastructures of urban poor leadership training from certificates to PhD, delivered in context at cost-effective levels.

I received this email last week:

> My first question is concerned about those Pastors who serve among the poor ; they want to study but don't have the Higher Level certificate (Advanced Level certificate). I am forced to address their problems.

> During the late years of 70's to 90's, Uganda as a country faced several challenges of disasters which brought that generation into severe poverty and the country went backwards in achieving education qualifications, yet many are in ministry. The 1979's war was accompanied by 1980-1986's war. In the late years of 1980 and early years of 1990's, the environmental disasters swept all sambas of coffee, cassava, and other cash crops and people were trailed in severe poverty. Uganda as a country missed a generation of educated people during that time.

> Many of these are Pastors who lack academic qualifications to pursue MA in Urban Leadership and we have many in our team. Is there any step taken to help these pastors?

> Referring to the above question, last week but one, we attended a meeting headed by one well known pastor. Out of many issues he addressed, he talked about pastors who lack academic qualifications that the government want to sue them out of ministry, but came out with a solution. He said, he is in touch with a school in the USA, they are going to offer Masters from their bible college and that they scheduled sub-course for ministers who don't have Advanced Level certificated, and this will enable them to continue for Masters degree program. We were over 500 pastors but all were happy for the idea. How can I advise pastors who have been walking with us but want to pursue their diplomas and degrees?

In essence, his cry is for a pathway. Or else a movement with some years of holistic training will now revert back into the spiritual academia of non-engaged evangelicalism based in the US.

Educational delivery infrastructure for transformation has to answer the following questions from the field:

1. Spirit-directed
2. Trust between participating entities within a consistent **global network.**
3. A philosophical **definition of the domain,** its content and limits precedes specifics of delivery.
4. A research-based coherent body of **desired content and outcomes.**
5. **Global validation** of vocational-style holistic ministry education at the

grassroots.

6. **Accreditation:** A progression of Acceptance of that global validation into national accreditation systems.

7. Diversified **adequate and sustainable resource base** to facilitate these processes at all levels.

8. Delivery Systems at the **level of cost** of the trainees context. This in turn modifies the content

9. Committed and trained educational **leadership** in each partner school institution or mission.

10. Accessible **Courseware platforms**

These are confirmed by evaluation against Andrew Sears' extensive analysis of the *Lean Start-up Hypothesis Testing on Christian Ecosystem.*[47] The following expands each of these:

Academic Quality

1. Spirit-Directed.

For I know that whatever God does endures forever. God has made it so in order that men fear before him (Ecc 3:14). Unless the Lord builds the house we labour in vain (Psa 127:1), for a man's mind plans his way, but the Lord directs his steps (Prov 19:21).

2. Trust within a Global Network

Working together has to be mutually beneficial, and be built on trust that is developed through serving each other in a mutuality.

This is only possible if such a network is resourced adequately enough to consistently bring leaders together to deliver progressive outcomes that contribute to the participants' felt needs.

3. Definition of the Domain

This has been done in a previoius chapter.

4. Desired Outcomes and Content

Defined outcomes determine content, and delivery style for training. Each partnering organization needs to define its outcomes, and these can be linked to outcomes on the infrastructure.

The content and outcomes for a master's' degree have been refined over these fifteen years and have been listed.[48]

Some initial feedback on the outcomes

for certificate and diploma training are listed on the next page, collated from multiple sources. It is expected that multiple models will develop and that cross-fertilization between these models is a desired process.

The need for Doctoral level training among MATUL graduates and adjunct professors is a crucial need as the quality of delivery in partner schools is crucial. A Doctorate in Transformational Leadership is proposed based on the British approach that a doctorate is independent research with a minimal taught courses.

5. Global Validation

Vocational training is validated by the employers confederations. They are the ones who define the skills needed. And they are integrally involved in the design of delivery.

The recommendations here are to utilise the concept of the NZQA framework (there are similar frameworks in vocational training in Britain and Australia). This consists of 9 levels of education, where modules between institutions can be validated on their system as at an equivalent level, and equivalent quality. There are progressions in this model from certificate to diploma to bachelors to master's to doctorate level education. Ways of defining outcomes at each level are clearly differentiated. It is recommended we utilize definitions derived from discussions on Bloom's taxonomy.[49]

6. Accreditation

Each country has its own accreditation systems, so this has been essential for partners to modify the core concepts to fit with their own context.

.

Commitment to evaluation is an essential concept for quality education. The concept of outside evaluation consumes enormous resources, and is more expensive than most programs can sustain. The alternative is a dual level:.

1. involvement of the participants in the

program and course design itself. They can best evaluate much of it. This is part of what is known as lean start up design.

2. The commission includes leaders of urban poor movements in the ongoing evaluative processes, so that outcomes fit the need.

7. Resources.

Diversified, adequate and sustainable resource based must be adequate to reach 50,000 leaders at all these levels. What are the minimal and ideal requirements for this?

Resource Principles
- These must be sustainable.
- These must be de-centered and diversified for survival.
- No educational system among the poor is likely to be self-funding so these will depend on donors, including institutional, foundations, churches and individuals.

There are two levels at which resourcing is needed: the global infrastructural level and the local seminary/university level that need to be considered.

Global Infrastructural Development Costs: Almost all the costs of development of the MATUL and MATUL Commission have been funded by Urban Leadership Foundation, through raising grants yearly. The minimum necessary has been $25,000 per year for the gathering of the Urban Poor Leaders Training Commission. This is on top of the self-funding of staff. I have observed over the years that a six- person global team with publishing, website development skills, fund-raising, admin and event organization capacity and able to travel to 12 cities (5 continents) yearly to work with trainers is a viable unit that can deliver. The Director of such a process needs skills in fund-raising, access to wealthy countries, an organisational base willing to back such a venture, and capacity to recruit staff who will raise their own support.

Contributions Between Schools: At the outset the genius of the Training Commission has been that each school has been autonomous in its delivery of the MATUL.

Some looked to APU as an American University, to somehow fund third world development. that is a misunderstanding of how American corporations work - they can only do that which is under their control and which leads to their expansion of an income base. Supporting foreign university development does not lead to an expansion of these. Thus APU has little history of resourcing other works. But it does have capacity to pay for some partner processes. APU put in a small amount per year in travel for APU faculty to schools. As we placed APU students in partner sites, fees students paid for auditing local classes were supportive of the program. APU's top quality curriculum design processes also has enabled an environment that fostered course development, thus supporting the other schools in this academic way. So US participation has been positive but only marginally so.

Dependency: Thus no moneys were transferred to other schools for program development. This was less than what was desired by partners, but fostered mutuality not dependency. However, it did not provide sufficient capital for successful sustainable launches.

Critical External Capitalization: My observation is that funding for a MATUL administrator and recruiter in each school from the outside is necessary, since with every budget change, deans or presidents seek to eliminate this position. Then the lack of recruitment reduces the program to a level of not being viable. Conclusion: $3-5000 per year is critical for sustaining the startup of the program.

8. Level of Cost of the Trainees

The first step in design is to design at the cost level of the trainee. And for grassroots training of slum pastors that is either a negative number or a minimal fee that will not even support the local trainer. So despite the rather evil thesis of the book, *The Fortune at the Bottom of the Pyramid* (Prahalad, 2005), there is no money to be made from grassroots training. It will be done as a beneficence, and that depends on benefactors.

Internet Cafe Learning Centres
I received this note form one of our learning network leaders: *My last query is about studying online. Many pastors I have approached about this program say,they would like to join the program if allowed, but they lack gadgets for assessing the teachings. Some suggested, is it possible to have a learning centre, facilitated with computers or screens and internet? It is possible for them to schedule time for lessons? How would you advise me on this?*

John Edmiston has developed a process for accomplishing this. [50]

Lean Startup Design
The concept of a lean startup (Ries, 2011) is to garner feedback at each step of the development phase. Classic education defines the outcomes and course content usually based on past history of what has been taught. In the domain of Urban Poor Missiology we are defining a number of the fields of knowledge as we go. The students themselves have pro-actively been involved in the evolving program design. They own it! the MATUL itself is a lean start up.

Contrasting Masters/Doctorate and Certificate Level Models
Andrew Sears talks of the contrast between the *Best in the World* model and the *Long Tail* model for maximum volume distribution. [51] At a master's level, we have worked to design a best of in the world model. But at the certificate and diploma level, the objective is mass multiplication, at minimal cost to recipients, and using platforms accessible by cell-phone and internet cafe.

9. Leadership

Trained Leadership for Masters and Doctorates
The greatest constraint in working with each university has been the regular turnover of leadership. And with each change in dean, director, administrator or President, a radical change of direction of the program. Deans are usually selected by Presidents on the basis of personal trust. They are likely highly skilled but usually with no knowledge of the underlying values of the program. Similarly Program Directors often have been invited in because they have worked for a development agency, but this is not a community development degree, it is a degree in movement leadership that builds from holistic ministry, church growth and social entrepreneurship. Community Development is one element of this. Community Development workers are rarely able to train people in church growth or even conceptualize pastoral ministry dynamics.

Leadership and Slum Learning Networks
John Edmiston, global technology consultant on Cybermissions, speaks of how the internet can communicate knowledge, but transmission of spirituality and character require face-to-face mentoring. We have found that the development of learning networks is essential, lead by a motivated trainer. Such a person is the critical key to transforming the world-view and practice of the pastors and workers on the ground. Each learning network needs to become self-funding, such that the trainer is able to support himself.

10. Accessible Courseware Platforms

The key to all of this is for the Training Commission to become an organization of Industry Providers that defines outcomes and credits providers. That is the discussion in the next two chapters.

Lean Startups

garner feedback at

Each stage of development of

Each product.

The MATUL is a lean startup.

14
Platforms: Reproducing Urban Poor Missiological Education

Andrew Sears has done some significant thinking as to how to scale existing innovative approaches for training of the urban poor into the delivery to millions needed in the future. He bases this on computer or phone accessibility by the millions to the web. Our goal is more modest as the previous experiment indicates that while phones are available, smart phones are not a useful way of training leaders in the slums, and computer access is not available except to the leaders of the learning networks, so we have set a goal of getting materials and training systems to 5000 of these leaders. Their (these leaders) training of the workers is then face-to-face, with sheets of notes on each topic. There *felt need* is (1) for a structure, and (2) for some kind of credit.

The Problem: Lack of Kingdom Theology

There are multiple delivery systems currently out there to deliver pure Bible materials. There are few delivering effective training for urban poor pastors in the arenas that the pastors have identified as needed. The Bible they have received is full of magic, but not one engaged with the economic and social context. They experience among themselves a sense that there is more to Christianity than magic, but without mentoring, it is a long search to find the depth of the Kingdom of God in the scriptures.

The Disruptive Solution.

Our niche is that we have designed training from the slums (not from the spiritualised Christianity of the Western seminary). We have made this available to the Seminaries but we are not defined by the Seminaries.

Andrew's understanding of disruptive innovation is that they start with the simplest, least threatening existing systems and replace them with alternative approaches. Gradually such innovations, as they capture market, can be scaled up to higher levels. We are in a good position as we are at the bottom levels, and have content, and some experimentations with products - both success and failure.

The above approach makes good sense in the business world, where small ideas can be made income-generating. In the slums, we do not have that income base. So donor-based models will need to cover the constant expansion as a critical feature if one uses such a business model.

Andrew Sears explores scaling existing Christian

Dean and Students, Azusa Pacific University

educational delivery and locates them into a schemata broken into two future clusters:

1. Existing University structures (which are not sustainable nor accessible to the large number of the urban poor)
2. The innovative experiments that are occurring which can be expanded exponentially at the grass-roots.

Some elements in the new models are similar to what was developed in the New Zealand Qualifications Authority approach in New Zealand including:

Unbundling

While we need to design preferred pathways, modules can be unpacked from multiple sources within a framework to add up to a complete learning pathway towards a diploma or degree.

Alternative Credit Mechanisms

While existing seminaries have to accommodate to their national accreditation system, alternative credit by an industry-wide body globally is logical. That then has to gain credibility as a pathway to access the existing degrees for those who would go forward. Thus credits for certificates and diplomas (or other named credits) need to have **dual recognition**: by the industry and as part of a ladder into the academy, where desired. The first is the primary driver. The second greatly increases marketability and value. The first can be scaled rapidly, the latter is critical in expanding the academic field through practitioners who emerge as thinkers in the field with degrees.

Accredited Degree Pathways

The felt need in an email today from Africa expressed: *Our country went through many years of trauma where education was halted, so our older leaders want to earn their degrees, but do not have the basic high school graduation to even begin, even though we have done much training. What can we do to offer this accreditation?*

This is a question of a clear pathway from certificate and diploma, based on recognized skill sets, and competency outcomes that the "industry" deems important.

Professional Associations

Our critical future role as the Encarnação Alliance Training Commission includes being the industry professional association as advisory to the delivering institutions. Effectiveness requires buy-in from those institutions, and perception that a relationship to such a professional association is of benefit to the institution. The association has to have a solid financial basis for this to occur. It also has to have some kind of defined credit pathway for this to occur. This includes:.
- credits for courses and content
- ways of evaluating delivery quality by partnering institutions.

This cannot be onerous or interfere with national accrediting processes but, like the American Psychological Association, be accepted as professional and supplemental.

This follows normative practice in Vocational Education, where course design begins with the Professional Industry Association and these remain as advisory groups who maintain standards of what credits they need with schools and the accrediting system.

Research Methodology

As action-reflection community-based research, the final step is to make proposals back to the decision-makers. This is the theme of the next two chapters.

15
Proposal:
Scaling the Urban Poor Leaders' Straining Commission

Building from these past experiences; continuing to grow the existing relationships; reflecting on the literature; listening to the experts all lead to the following proposal for the Urban Leadership Training Commission.

We expand our network to include leadership and institutions that enable the following:.

1. We press on to the development of **pathways** with four levels
   - Mass multiplication at the grassroots of certificates. Four certificates become a diploma recognized by the commission or another body. This follows vocational training models.
   - A process where these feed into a Bachelors degree
   - A process where these feed into the MATUL for movement leaders
   - A Doctorate in Transformational Urban Leadership by an accredited university.

1.1. **Breadth:** This movement leadership training continues to cover the six movement leadership roles: apostle, prophet, evangelist, pastor, teacher, deacon/ess. The latter results in entrepreneurship and social entrepreneurship training. Thus Community Development falls as small section within the latter but must never become determinative of any degree offered under the commission. We are primarily engaged in apostolic movement leadership development. Nor is it a social work degree.

1.2. **Alternative Credits in a Bifocal Delivery Systems as an Industry Accrediiation Organization**. Mass multiplication of Vocational Training: At the certificate and diploma level we integrate delivery from multiple sources that meet our criteria for effective slum leader education. These we credit certificates from multiple sources internationally and diplomas where national accreditation processes allow.

1.3. Thus we become **an industry association**, that credits quality training by recognized providers. High Quality Academic training: at the MATUL and Doctoral levels we continue to work with existing institutions, who seek accreditation within their own national accreditation systems

1.4 To be industry recognized, the partnering educational institutions must be required to meet the requirements for consistent appointment of appropriate leadership and recruiters as part of their professional association obligations (i.e. to remain members they need to fulfil some minimal responsibilities for recruitment, faculty leadership, admin leadership, holistic apostolic movement leadership (vs community development or Social work leadership) and content).

2. The Urban Poor Leaders Training Commission upgrades from a network of innovators to a global Industry *Professional Association* with paid (according to country income levels) membership at four levels:
- Urban poor movement leaders.
- Learning network trainers.
- BTUL, CTUL and MATUL, DTUL program directors.
- Associate Members? Community Development NGO leaders may become associate members, but may not make up more than 30% of the above membership, due to their historic tendency through their easy access to money and their administrative skills to take over the apostolic processes.
- .

This requires formalizing membership, fees and responsibilities.
- The position of Commission coordinator that has been empty for some years needs filling.
- The Coordinator must have administrative capacity for implementation and fund-raising capacity funding the core leadership gatherings, website development, and some critical support for partnering organizations and personal support.
- The chairman-innovator remains responsible for envisioning and process conceptualisation and some fund-raising.
- Core decisions are processed with a leadership team drawn from partner schools.

3. *Infrastructural Base*: The commission which legally resides under Urban Leadership Foundation Trust in New Zealand is ideally backed onto a partnership, perhaps as an Institute connected to a larger institution as a skunk-works (a *skunk-works* is an experimental section of a company exploring new innovations, it is hidden, off to the side and protected). Five options need to be considered.
- The experimentation with US Educational Institutions as a base does not indicate these as good options as all resources are analysed in terms of expansion of the US business model and money

flows to 40% administration.
- A third-world institution may be an option, but this requires it to have significant resources and accreditation.
- Exploration of an existing global non-profit could be considered. Their lack of theological commitment to movement leadership development and focus on projects-based community development likely precludes this. (i.e. their diaconal calling to transfer resources does not predict a theological or practical commitment to apostolic development).
- A denominational base may be an option, provided they see significance in serving the wider body of Christ.
- In the end, we keep coming back to developing one independently, but struggle with resourcing.

4. *Diversified Funding Model:* Each partner carries responsibility to fund its own delivery of training within its existing structure.
- This does not preclude the Commission from seeking funding for grants for *capitalization* of processes, such as an internet cafe for a learning network, or the initial funding of a recruiter/admin assistant from within the urban poor pastors networks for the MATUL.
- It does preclude the Commission from seeking funding for ongoing sustainability.
- The Commission raises funding for Commission gatherings and grants for some travel and accommodation, but members contribute for their costs.
- Members pay a membership fee to the commission adjusted for economic levels, similar to the manner of Micah Network, ranging from $500 for US Entities to $10 for a local Indian or Ugandan learning network.

16

From Slum Leadership to Post-Postmodern City Transformation

The preceding discussion has focussed on ministry training. This enables a wedge for the expansion into multiple dimensions of the Kingdom and its engagement with Society

Parallel MA in Public Policy

The MATUL as entrance point in theological education. Complementing the MATUL is the need for education for transformation from the top. This can be done in cities where there is a significant Christian population.

The natural expansion is in the realm. of social entrepreneurship. But that presupposes management courses.

The second direction is expansion of education from church-based preschool to schools to vocational schools. Teacher education becomes a crucial need.

The third is advocacy into policy making dimensions in areas of community health, land rights, and education.

This might best begun perhaps as a *Masters in Religion and Public Policy* or a *Doctorate in Urban Leadership*. This could be crafted around similar themes as the MATUL but with a target to upper level executives.

Multiplying Urban Institutes

All of these logically fit into Urban Institutes to be developed city by city. Such an institute to be funded by seminar type weekends for each arena of policy-making.

The Masters for upper level policy-making should be able to fund the MA in Transformational Urban Leadership for slum workers.

A good model for this has been Doug Hall and the Emmanuel Gospel Centre in Boston.

It is debatable as to whether these are best as stand alone centres for Urban Culture and Society, places where people of all faiths can come and debate policy in the light of Biblical theologyin seminars, or backed onto Bible schools or as one of the Institutes in the formation of Christian Universities.

Five Phases of Urban Transformation

All of this fits with the fourth of five phases of 50 years of Urban Transformation that I laid out in the 1990's for the global missions community as I lead the AD 2000 Cities track globally.

1.   Mobilize catalytic teams to global

slums (1.3 Billion) from West (70's-90's).

2. Catalyse indigenous movements of 10,000 disciples, churches, Bible school in slums of each of 6600 cities (90's-2015).

3. Movements engage in significant transformational of slums (95-2020).

4. As a result, movements for urban transformation sparked among the urban elites (2000-2025).

5. Transformation of culture, philosophies and structures of conurbanizations (2020-2050) to welcome back the King. [52].

This upper level of urban policy-making education is feasible, where there are sufficient numbers of believers, or where there is an openness to Christian education, such as in Hindu India. Ultimately the multiplication of Christian Universities is a crucial need. Urban Institutes are a significant step in that direction, perhaps more logical than shifting Bible Schools into becoming Universities or perhaps a first step in those progression.

There have been attempts to do this in some places. Wider coalitions are needed among the Urban Missions schools to make this a reality.

Hidden Beauty of the Developed Slum. Photo: Adobe Stock.

Finale

Hong Kong Panorama. Photo: Adobe Stock

The Word keeps echoing. The Spirit keeps hovering and turning chaos into structure.

Across the deserts of North Africa and Saudi Arabia, Iraq and Iran, glittering mega-cities rise from sand. In China in the last decades, 1000 new cities have been constructed as part of their ten year plans. The cities of the West have become conurbations - Greater Los Angeles and its five counties stretches across 183 cities.

> *Through him all things were made; without him, nothing was made that has been made (John 1:3).*

He is the urbanizing God. Since my childhood, over 67 years, I have watched a few mega-cities become a fire of light around the world in these great conurbations of over 20,000 mega-cities over 1,000,000. Places of Life and Light. For he is at the centre of these cities, whether acknowledged or not.

> *In him was life, and that life was the light of mankind. The light shines in the darkness, and the darkness has not overcome it (1:4).*

These cities are built in a great mixture of light and life-giving and intense darkness of oppression, injustice, exploitation and poverty. The slums are both the ultimate expression of all that darkness and the expression of the irrational hope of the migrant peasant. It is in revealing Christ into these cities that brings the true light and life. In the past pages we have reflected on multiple initiatives that lay the foundations of placing Christ at the centre of the urban millenium.

The true light that gives light to everyone was coming into the world. He was in the world, and though the world was made through him, the world did not recognize him (1:10).

That light is manifest in the truth of appropriate Christian educational structures, which train believers to see him at the centre of all the structures of the cities, the integrator, the reconciler, the source of life. It is manifest as some go out to multiply movements of economic discipleship, built on the spiritual foundations of church growth. And others in social movements for change towards the Kingdom of God.

In these pages, I have cried out like a voice in the desert, for the advance of that Light and Life in educational programs at the beginning of the urban millennium. Programs that impact both the slums and the centres of the city. Some things have succeeded, many have failed. Many thousands have been trained in the holistic Kingdom of God in such ways that they are transforming their arenas of society and the slums. This analysis has been somewhat personal story, somewhat structural. Perhaps in the next in this series, others involved in delivery will tell the deeper content of the global education discussed here.

As we see the impending signs of his return to establish his reign on earth and beyond it the Holy City, may we be found at work, laying the foundations of these cities, training oaks of righteousness, servants on whom he can depend to rule when he comes, perhaps this year, perhaps next, perhaps in a decade, though with the apostle John we pray, "Come Lord Jesus!"

Smokey Mountain: Garbage Dump and Squatter Area, Manila. Photo: Viv Grigg, 1980

Future Smokey Mountain? Is Dehumanized Urbanism the Ultimate Answer? Photo: Adobe Stock

References

- Alinsky, S. (1969). *Reveille for Radicals*. New York: Vintage Books.
- Bakke, R. (1997). *A Theology As Big As the City*. Downers Grove, IL: IVP Press.
- Batty, M., & Longley, P. (1994). *Fractal Cities*. San Diego: Academic Press.
- Berger, P. (1987). *The Capitalist Revolution: Fifty Propositions About Prosperity, Equality and Liberty*. New York: Basic Books.
- Berger, P. L., Berger, B., & Kellner, H. (1973). *The Homeless Mind: Modernization and Consciousness*. New York: Random House.
- Bessenecker, S. (2006). *The New Friars: The Emerging Movement Serving the World's Poor*. Downers Grove, IL: IVP.
- Bessenecker, S. (Ed.) (2010). *Living Mission: The Vision and Voices of New Friars*. Downers Grove, WI: Intervarsity Press.
- Bevans, S. B., S.V.D. (1996). *Models of Contextual Theology*. Maryknoll: Orbis.
- Book-Satterlee, K. (2013). *Out of the Cloister and into the Streets: Two Partnership Models of Integrated Praxiological Andragogy in Cross-Cultural Urban Ministry*. William Carey International Development Journal, 2(2).
- Boud, D, & John Garrick, ed., (1999). Competency-Based Learning. *Understanding Learning at Work*. London: Routlege.
- Boyer, E. (1990). *Scholarship Reconsidered: Priorities of the Professoriate*. Carnegie Foundation.
- Brueggeman, W. (1977). *The Land*. Philadelphia: Fortress Press.
- ---. (1997). *Theology of the Old Testament: Testimony, Dispute, Advocacy*. Minneapolis: Fortress Press.
- Busseau, D., & Samuel, V. (1998). *How Then Should We Lend?* Oxford: Opportunity International.
- Catherwood, S. F. (c1967). *The Christian in Industrial Society*. London: IVP.
- Childs, Brevards. (1970). *Biblical Theology in Crisis*. Philadelphia: Westminster.
- Conn, Harvey. (1984). *Eternal Word and Changing Worlds*. Phillipsburg, NJ: P & R Publishing.
- Conn, H., & Ortiz, M. (2001). *Urban Ministry*. Downers Grove: Intervarsity Press.
- Craig, J. (1998). *Servants Among the Poor*. Manila: OMF Publishers.
- Davey, C. J. (1960). *Kagawa of Japan*. Nashville: Abingdon.
- de Santa Ana, J. (1982). *Towards a Church of the Poor*. Geneva: WCC.
- de Soto, H. (2002). *The Other Path: An Economic Answer to Terrorism* (J. Abbott, Trans.). New York: Basic Books, original edition Harper & Row.
- Duncan, M. (1996). *Costly Mission: Following Christ into the Slums*. Monrovia: MARC.
- Ellul, J. (1997). *The Meaning of the City*. Greenwood, SC: Attic Press.
- Fackre, G. (1983). Narrative Theology: An Overview. *Interpretation*. 37(No. 4 (October)), pp. 340-353.
- Fanon, F. (1986). *The Wretched of the Earth*. New York: Grove.
- Freire, Paulo. (1986). *Pedagogy of the Oppressed* (M. B. Ramos, Trans.). New York: Continuum.
- Gramsci, Antonio (1982). *Selections from the Prison Books*. Lawrence and Wishart.
- Grant, G. (1986). *In the Shadow of Plenty*. Fort Worth, TX: Dominion Press.
- Griffith, B. (1984). *The Creation of Wealth*. London: Hodder & Stoughton.
- Gardner, H. (1993). *Creating Minds*. New York: Basic Books.
- Gerlach, L., & Hine, V. (1970). *People, Power, Change: Movements of Social Transformation*. Indiana: Bobs Merrill.
- Glassick, C. E., Huber, M. T., & Maeroff, G. I. (1997). *Scholarship Assessed: Evaluation of the Professoriate*. San Francisco: Jossey-Bass.
- Fackre, G. (1983). Narrative Theology: An Overview. *Interpretation*, 37(No. 4 (October)), 340-353.
- Frantz Fanon. (1963). *The Wretched of the Earth*. Grove Press.
- Festinger, Leon. (1959). *A Theory of Cognitive Dissonance*. London: Tavistock.

- Gleick, J. (1987). *Chaos: Making a New Science*. New York: Penguin.
- Grigg, Viv. (2000). *Creating an Auckland Business Theology*. Auckland: Urban Leadership Foundation.
- ___. (1985/2004). *Biblical Reflections on Land and Land Rights*. Auckland: Urban Leadership Foundation.
- ___. (1992/2004). *Cry of the Urban Poor*. London: Authentic Press.
- ___. (1997b). Transforming the Soul of the Nation. In B. Patrick (Ed.), *Vision New Zealand Congress (1997)*. Auckland: Vision New Zealand.
- ___. (2009). *The Spirit of Christ and the Postmodern City: Transformative Revival Among Auckland's Evangelicals and Pentecostals*. Lexington, KY: Emeth Press and Auckland: Urban Leadership Foundation.
- ___. (2009). Transformational Conversations: Hermeneutic for a Postmodern City. *The Spirit of Christ and the Postmodern City: Transformative Revival Among Auckland's Evangelicals and Pentecostals*. Lexington, KY: Asbury: Emeth Press & Auckland: Urban Leadership Foundation.
- ___. (2010). *Conversations on Economic Discipleship* (5 ed.). Wellington, New Zealand: Urban Leadership Foundation.
- ___. (2012). (Nov). *Uma igreja relevante encarnada: o reino, a igreja e a terra*. (The relevant church, the reign, the church and the land). Plenary at the Conferência Missionária do Estado de São Paulo (CMESP), Rio de Janiero, Brazil.
- ___. (2010). Hovering Spirit, Creative Voice, Empowered Transformation: A Retrospective. In *Living Mission*, Scott Bessnecker Ed. IVP Books. pp 23-35. (2012). Reprinted in *The New Urban World Journal*. Vol 1:1. Stephen Burris, Ed. Bangkok: International Society of Urban Mission. www.newurbanworld.org
- ___. (2014). CMESP. *O Reino de Deus e Economia Solidaria*. Plenary at the Conferência Missionária do Estado de São Paulo (CMESP), Rio de Janiero, Brazil.
- Grigg, Viv., Kuini Siuelu ed., Asenla Bendang ed., Murray Dillner, Stephen Saddiq, & Park, J. (Oct 27-28 2000). *Ethnic and Indigenous Peoples Story-Telling Hui: A journey towards indigenous and ethnic theologies in Auckland*. Paper presented at the Ethnic and Indigenous Peoples Story-Telling Hui:, Onehunga High School Marae.
- Gronlund, Norman and Susan Brookhart. (2008) *Writing Instructional Objectives*. 8th Edn. Pearson.
- Hagner, D. (1998). *The New Testament and Criticism: Looking at the Twenty-first Century*. Theology, News and Notes, 7-10.
- Hall, B. P. (1995). *Values Shift: A Guide to Personal and Organizational Transformation*. Twin Lights Publishing.
- Rob Hay, Valerie Lim, Detlef Blocher, & et al. (2007). *Worth Keeping*. William Carey Library: World Evangelical Alliance
- Hayes, J. (2006). *sub-Merge*. Ventura: Regal.
- Hengel, M. (1974). *Property and Riches in the Early Church*. Philadelphia: Fortress Press.
- Hoffer, E. (1966). *The True Believer*. 49 East 33rd Street, New York, New York, 10016: Harper & Row Publishers.
- Holland, & Henriott. (1974). *Social Analysis: Linking Faith and Justice*. Orbis.
- Illich, I. (1957). *Missionary Poverty*. Doulos Christou Press.
- Iremonger, F.A. (1948). *William Temple, Archbishop of Canterbury: His Life and Letters*. Oxford: Oxford Press.
- Jack, K. (2010). *The Sound of World's Colliding*. Phnom Phen: Hawaii Printing House.
- Kagawa, T. (1936). *Brotherhood Economics*. New York and London: Harper and Brothers.
- Keller, T. (2012). *Center Church*. Grand Rapids, MI: Zondervan.
- Kuhn, Thomas. (1962/1970). *The Structure of Scientific Revolutions*. Chicago: University of Chicago Press.
- Ladd, G. E. (1959). *The Gospel of the Kingdom*. Grand Rapids: Eerdmans.
- Leffel, G. P. (2007). *Faith Seeking Action: Mission, Social Movements and the Church in Motion*. Lanham, MD: Scarecrow Press.
- Libanio, J. B. (2001). *As Lógicas da Cidade: O Impacto Sobre a Fé e Sob o Impacto da Fé*. (City Structures: The Impact of Faith and Under the Impact of Faith). São Paulo: Edições Loyola.
- Lynch, F. (c1979). *Lowland Filipino Values*. Manila: Ateneo de Manila.
- McLaren, P. (1999). A Pedagogy of Possibility: Reflecting on Paulo Freire's Politics of Education: In Memory of Paulo Freire. *Educational Researcher*, 28(2), 49-56.
- MacIntyre, A. (1988). *Whose Justice? Which Rationality?* Notre Dame, IN: University of Notre Dame Press.
- Marsden, George. (1997). *The Outrageous Idea of Christian Scholarship*. Oxford: Oxford University Press.
- Murphy, N. (1997). *Anglo-American Postmodernity*. Boulder, CO: Westview Press.
- Newbigin, L. (1981). Politics and the Covenant. *Theology*, LXXXIV(Sept 1981 no 701).
- Novak, M. (1982). *The Spirit of Democratic Capitalism*. New York: Touchstone, Simon and Schuster.
- Pierson, P. (1998). *History of Theology of Evangelical Awakenings* Course Notes. Pasadena: Fuller Theological

Seminary, School of World Missions.

- Prahalad, (2005). *The Fortune at the Bottom of the Pyramid: Eradicating Poverty Through Profits.* Wharton School of Business.
- Quine, W. V. O., & Ullian, J. S. (1978). *The Web of Belief* (2nd ed.). New York: Random House.
- Brother Roger. (1981). *Parable of community: The rule and other basic texts of Taize.* Seabury Press.
- Rutherford, S., & Arora, S. (2009). *The Poor and their Money.* Warwickshire: Practical Action Publishing.
- Sabatier, P., & Sweney, J. M. (2003 (1894)). *The Road to Assisi: The Essential Biography of St Francis.* MA: Paraclete Press.
- Salvatierra, A., & Heltzel, P. (2014). *Faith-Rooted Organizing: Mobilizing the Church in the Service of the World.* Downers Grove, IL: IVP.
- Santos, M. (1979). *The Shared Space* (C. Gerry, Trans.). London and New York: Methuen.
- Scott, W. (1980). *Bring Forth Justice: A Contemporary Perspective on Mission.* Grand Rapids: Eerdmans.
- Gutierrez, G. (1973/1988). *A Theology of Liberation* (Sr. Caridad Inda & J. Eagleson, Trans. With new introduction, 1988 ed.). New York: Orbis Books and London: SCM Press.
- Ledgerwood, J. (1999). *Microfinance Handbook: An Institutional and Financial Perspective.* Washington: The International Bank for Reconstruction and development/World Bank.
- McClelland, D. C. (1964). Business Drive and National Achievement. In Amitai Etzioni & E. Etzioni (Eds.), *Social Change* (Vol. XL, pp. 165-178). New York and London: Basic Books.
- Osborne, G. R. (1991). *The Hermeneutical Spiral: A Comprehensive Introduction to Biblical Interpretation.* Downers Grove, IL: IVP Press.
- Perdue, L. G. (1994). *The Collapse of History: Restructuring Old Testament Theology.* Minneapolis: Fortress Press.
- Quine, W. V. O., & Ullian, J. S. (1978). *The Web of Belief* (2nd ed.). New York: Random House.
- Ries, E. (2011). *The Lean Startup: How Today's Entrepreneurs Use Continuous Innovation to Create Radically Successful Businesses.* Crown Business.
- Savicevic, Dusan. (1996). *Adult Education: From Practice to Theory Building.* Peter Lang Publishing.
- Salvatierra. Alexia. (2014). *Faith-Rooted Organizing.* IVP.
- Smith, M. K. (1999, 2011). 'What is praxis?' in *The Encyclopaedia of Informal Education.* [http://infed.org/mobi/what-is-praxis/. Retrieved: August 5, 2018.
- Snyder, H. (1997). *A Kingdom Manifesto.* Eugene, OR: Wipf and Stock Publishers (1985 edn. by IVP).
- Taylor, Louise. Rethinking priorities: Making time for transformational conversations [online]. *Early Education*, Vol. 50, Spring/Summer 2011: 15-18. Availability: <https://search.informit.com.au/documentSummary;dn=716339874979724;res=IELNZC> ISSN: 1172-9112. [cited 05 Jul 18].
- Sears, Andrew. (2018). *GC4 and Alternative Models for Christian Accreditation for the Majority World*, slide 84. Slideshare. Accessed July 7, 2018.
- ---. (2018). Personal Strategy Principles from Case Studies. *Disruptive Innovation.* Udemy slide presentation, Accessed July 7, 2018.
- Tippett, A. (1971). *People Movements in Southern Polynesia.* Chicago: Moody Bible Institute.
- UN-Habitat. (2007). *State of the World's Cities: Global Report on Human Settlements 2007.* Earthscan Publications.
- Van Engen, C. (1996). *Mission on the Way: Issues in Mission Theology.* Grand Rapids, MI: Baker Book House.
- Vanhoozer, K. J. (1995). Mapping Evangelical Theology in a Post-modern World. *Trinity Journal,* 16.
- Vela, Jane. (2002) *Learning to Listen, Learning to Teach: The Power of Dialogue in Educating Adults* 2nd Edition. Jossey-Bass.
- Vos, J. (c1995). *Breaking Down the Walls.* South Africa: Thummin Printing.
- Winters, R. (1974). *The Two Structures of God's Redemptive Mission.* Missiology, II, No. 1, Jan. 1974.
- Wink, J. (2005). *Critical Pedagogy.* Pearson.
- Yunus, M. (2003). *Banker to the Poor: Micro-Lending and the Battle Against World Poverty.* New York: Perseus Books.

Movement Leadership

- Aldrich, J. (1992). *Prayer Summits.* Portland, OR, Multnomah Press.
- Alinsky, S. (1969). *Reveille for Radicals.* New York, Vintage Books.
- Allen, R. (1927/1956). *The Spontaneous Expansion of the Church.* London, World Dominion

Press.

- Berg, M. and P. Pretiz (1996). *Spontaneous Combustion: Grass Roots Christianity,* Latin American Style. Pasadena, William Carey Library.
- Berkhof, H. (1962/1977). *Christ and the Powers.* Scottsdale, PA, Herald Press.
- Bessenecker, S. (2006). *The New Friars: The Emerging Movement Serving the World's Poor.* Downers Grove, IL, IVP.
- Cannistraci, D. and C. P. Wagner (1998). *Apostles and the Emerging Apostolic Movement.* Ventura, Gospel Light.
- Davey, Cyril. (2000). *Saint in the Slums: Kagawa of Japan,* Jersey City: Parkwest Publications.
- Dawson, J. (1989). *Taking Our Cities for God.* Lake Mary, FL, Creation House.
- --- (1996a). *Healing America's Wounds.* Ventura, Regal Books.
- Dennison, J. (1999). *City Reaching: On the Road to Community Transformation.* Pasadena, William Carey Library.
- Freire, P. (1986). *Pedagogy of the Oppressed.* New York, Continuum.
- Fromm, Erich. (1983) *Escape from Freedom.* AVon Books.
- Garrison, David. (1999). *Church Planting Movements.* Richmond, VA: Office of Overseas Operations, International Mission Board of the Southern Baptist Convention.
- Garvin, M. (1998). *The Divine Art of Networking.* Gordon St, Poatina, Tasmania: Whitestone, Fusion Australia.
- Gerlach, L.P. & Hein, V.H. (1970). *People, Power, Change: Movements of Social Transformation.* NY: Bobbs-Merrill Co.
- Greenleaf, R. K. (1977). *Servant Leadership: A Journey into the Nature of Legitimate Power and Authority.* NY, Paulist.
- Grigg, V. (1986). *SERVANTS: A Protestant Missionary Order With Vows of Simplicity and Non-Destitute Poverty.* Auckland, Urban Leadership Foundation.
- --- (1993). "Intercessors and Cosmic Urban Spiritual Warfare." *International Journal of Frontier Missions* 10:4(Oct 1993).
- --- (2004a). *Companion to the Poor.* Monrovia, CA, Authentic Media (revised and updated), originally Abatross: Sydney (1984), revised MARC: Monrovia (1990)).
- --- (2004b). *Cry of the Urban Poor.* London, Authentic Press.
- --- (2007). *Transforming Cities: An Urban Leadership Guide.* Auckland, Urban Leadership Foundation, P.O. Box 20-524, Glen Eden, Auckland.
- --- (2009). *The Spirit of Christ and the Postmodern City: Transformative Revival Among Auckland's Evangelicals and Pentecostals.* Lexington, KY, Emeth Press and Auckland: Urban Leadership Foundation.
- Hoffer, E. (1951). *The True Believer.* New York and London, Harper & Row.
- Martin, D. (1990). *Tongues of Fire: The Explosion of Protestantism in Latin America.* Cambridge, MA, Basil Blackwell.
- Maslow, A. H. (1954). *Motivation and Personality.* New York: Harper and Row.
- Massey, J. (1998). *Christianity Among the Dalits in North India with Special Reference to the Punjab. Christianity in India: Search for Liberation and Identity.* F. Hrangkhuma. Delhi, ISPCK CMS.
- McAlpine, T. H. (1991). *Facing the Powers: What are the Options?* Monrovia, MARC
- McGavran, D. (1970). *Understanding Church Growth.* Grand Rapids, Eerdmans.
- Mellis, C. (1976). *Committed Communities.* Pasadena, William Carey Library Publishers.
- Neighbour, R. J. (1995). *Where Do We Go From Here? A Guidebook to the Cell Church.* Singapore, Touch Publications, Touch Resources #06-00, 66/68 East Coast Road, Singapore 1542.
- Petersen, D. (1996). *Not by Might Nor by Power: A Pentecostal Theology of Social Concern in Latin America.* Oxford, Regnum Books.
- Rogers, E. M. (2003). *Diffusion of Innovations,* Free Press.
- Schwarz, C. A. (1996). *Natural Church Development; A Guide to Eight Essential Qualities of Healthy Churches.* St. Charles, IL, ChurchSmart Resources.
- Silvoso, E. (1994). *That None Should Perish.* Ventura, Regal Books.
- Tippett, A. (1971). *People Movements in Southern Polynesia.* Chicago: Moody Bible Institute.
- Troeltsch, E. (1911/1960). *The Social Teaching of the Christian Churches.* New York, Harper and Row.
- Wallace, A. F.C. (2003). *Revitalization Movements.* In R. S. Grumet (Ed.), Revitalizations and Mazeways, pp. 9-29. Lincoln and London: University of Nebraska Press.
- Wallis, A. (2005). *In the Day of They Power,* Revival Library. 2005.
- Winter, R. (1974, January). *The Two Structures of God's Redemptive Mission.* Missiology, II, No. 1.
- Zalenski, Abraham. (2005). Managers and Leaders: Are they Different? *Harvard Business Review on the Mind of the Leader.* pp. 73-78.

Urban Spirituality

A selection of books on different perspectives of spirituality contributing to the field of urban poor spirituality:

Pentecostal Spirituality

- Murphy, Ed. (2003). *The Handbook of Spiritual Warfare.* (revised and updated) Nashville: Thomas Nelson.

Incarnational Mission

- Bessenecker, Scott. (2006). *The New Friars: The Emerging Movement Serving the World's Poor.* Downers Grove, IL: IVP.
- Grigg, Viv. (2004). *Companion to the Poor.* Monrovia, CA: Authentic Media (revised and updated).

Catholic Liberation

- Gutierrez, Gustavo. (1984). *We Drink from our Own Wells: The Spiritual Journey of a People.* New York: Orbis Books; London: SCM Press.

A Comprehensive Textbook

- Boa, Ken. (2001). *Conformed to his Image.* Grand Rapids: Zondervan..

Theology of the Holy Spirit

- Kärkäinen, Veli-Matti. (2002). *Pneumatology: The Holy Spirit in Ecumenical, International and Contextual Persectives.* Grand Rapids: Baker.

Disciplines

- The Navigators. (n.d.) *The Topical Memory System.* Colorado Springs: Nav Press.
- Examen Exercises
- Brother Lawrence of the Resurrection. (1982). *The Practice of the Presence of God.* Whitaker House.
- Grigg, Viv. (1980). *The Disciple and Self: Facets of the Inner Core of Selflessness from the Beatitudes.* Reach Communique. Urban Leadership Foundation.
- ---. (1985). *The Lifestyle and Values of Servants.* Auckland: Urban Leadership Foundation.
- ---. (2004) To Have or Not to Have. *Companion to the Poor.* Authentic
- Foster, Richard. (1998). *Celebration of Discipline.* New York: HarperCollins..

Cross-Cultural Spirituality

- Abeledo, Yago. (2002). The Slums: The Challenge of a Crucified People. In Franceso Pierli and Yago Abeledo (Ed.), T*he Slums:A Challenge to Evangelizatio*n (pp. 109-132). Daughters of St Paul, P.O. Box 49026, 00100 Nairobi GPO: Paulinas Publications Africa.
- Brewster, E. T. and E. S. Brewster (1982). *Bonding and the Missionary Task.* 135 North Oakland Box #114 Pasadena California 91101, Lingua House.
- Capaque, George N. (c2000) *Pagbubukas-Loob: A Filipino Evangelical Theology of Spirituality.* Excerpt from PhD Thesis, Asian Theological Seminary.
- Cone, James H. (2005). God and Black Suffering. *The Spirituals and the Blues. An Interpretation.* New York: Orbis Press.
- Flavier, Juan M. (1974). Ka Berong, Albularyo. In *My Friends in the Barrios.* Manila: New Day Publishers.
- Grigg, Viv. (2005). An Insider's Perspective. In *Cry of the Urban Poor.* GA, USA: Authentic Media. ch 15.
- Illich, Ivan. (2010). Missionary Poverty. *The Church, Change and Community Development.* Doulos Christou Press. http://douloschristou.com/illich accessed Nov 19, 2010.
- Jocano, F. Landa. (1980). The Coming of the Gods. In *Outline of Philippine Mythology.* Manila: Centro Escolar University Research and Development Center.
- Ligo, Arche. (1993). Liberation Themes in Philippine Popular Religiosity: A Case Study. *Voices from the Third World,* XVI (2), 117-142.

Justice Spirituality

- Gutierrez, Gustavo. (1984). *We drink from our own wells: The Spiritual Journey of a People.* Orbis Books.
- Salvatierra. Alexia. (2014). *Faith-Rooted Organizing.* IVP.
- Stassen, Glen (2008) *Just Peacemaking.* Cleveland: Pilgrim.
- Smith, James K.A. (2017) *Awaiting the King: Reforming Public Theology.* Baker Academic.
- Tizon, Al. (2018) *Whole and Reconciled.* Baker Academic.

Phenomenology

- Grigg, Viv. (2005). Works of the Spirit of God. In *Cry of the Urban Poor.* GA, USA: Authentic Media.

- Koch, Kurt. (1994). Pastoral Cases from the Field of Occultism. *Christian Counselling and Occultism* (fr German, Trans.). Grand Rapids: Kregel.
- Murphy, Ed. (1996). Six Sin Areas and Possible Demonisation of Christians. *The Handbook of Spiritual Warfare*. Nashville: Thomas Nelson..

Apostolic Orders

- Bessenecker, Scott. (2006). Voluntary Poverty of God. *The New Friars: The Emerging Movement Serving the World's Poor.* Downers Grove, IL: IVP.
- Biot, F., O.P. (1963). *The Rise of Protestant Monasticism.* 1120 N. Calvert St., Baltimore, Maryland, 21202: Helicon Press Inc.
- Sabatier, Paul & Sweney, Jon M. (2003 (1894)). *The Road to Assisi: The Essential Biography of St Francis.* MA: Paraclete Press.
- Bonaventure. (1978). *The Soul's Journey into God, The Tree of Life, The Life of Saint Francis* (E. Cousins, Trans.). New York: Paulist Press.
- Grigg, V. (1986). *SERVANTS: A Protestant Missionary Order with Vows of Simplicity and Non-Destitute Poverty.* Auckland: Urban Leadership Foundation.

Spiritual Conflict

- Boa, Ken. (2001). Warfare with the Flesh. *Conformed to his Image.* Grand Rapids: Zondervan. BV4501.2 .B592 2001, ISBN 031023848X $18.47 (A)
- Grigg, V. (1993). Intercessors and Cosmic Urban Spiritual Warfare. *International Journal of Frontier Missions.* 10:4(Oct 1993).

Self-Analysis

- Breen, M. (2002). Fivefold Ministries. In *The Apostle's Notebook.* Eastbourne, England, pp. 161-171, 220 ISBN 1842910078 $150.90 (AU)
- Cox, Harvey. (1995).Your Daughters Shall Prophesy. *Fire from Heaven: The Rise of Pentecostal Spirituality and the Reshaping of Religion in the Twenty-First Century.* Reading, MA: Addison-Wesley. 161-184.
- Sandford, John and Paula. (1985). The Forgotten Functions of Our Spirit. In *Healing the Wounded Spirit* (pp. 3-26). Tulsa, OK: Victory House, Inc.

Timing and Seasons

- Grigg. (2005). Group Structures for Squatter Churches. In *Cry of the Urban Poor.* GA, USA:

Authentic Media. ch 13.
-

Urban Contextual Spirituality

- Hanks, Thomas. (1984). Basic Old Testament Vocabulary of Oppression. *God So Loved the Third World.* Maryknoll, Orbis Books. pp3-25.
- Grigg, Viv. (2009). *The Holy Spirit and the Postmodern City: Transformative Revival Among Auckland's Evangelicals and Pentecostals.* Emeth Press.

Incarnation in the Slums

Some recent books by incarnational urban poor missions leaders.

- Barker, A. (2014). *Risky Compassion.* Melbourne: ISUM.
- Barker, A. (2009). *Make Poverty Personal: Taking the Poor as Seriously as the Bible Does*: Baker Books.
- Bessenecker, S. (2006). *The New Friars: The Emerging Movement Serving the World's Poor.* Downers Grove, IL: IVP.
- Bessenecker, S. (2005). *Quest for Hope in the Slum Community.* Waynesborough, GA: Authentic.
- Bessenecker, S. (Ed.) (2010). *Living Mission: The Vision and Voices of New Friars.* Downers Grove, WI: Intervarsity Press.
- Craig, J. (1998). *Servants Among the Poor.* Manila: OMF Publishers.
- Duncan, M. (1996). *Costly Mission: Following Christ into the Slums.* Monrovia: MARC.
- Greenfield, C. (2007). *The Urban Halo: A Story of Hope for Orphans of the Poor.* London: Authentic.
- Greenfield, C. (2016). *Subversive Jesus: An Adventure in Justice, Mercy, and Faithfulness in a Broken World*: Zondervan.
- Hayes, J. (2006). *sub-Merge.* Ventura: Regal.
- Smith, A. (2012). *Living in the Neighbourhood.* Pomona: Servant Partners.
- Vos, J. (c1995). *Breaking Down the Walls.* South Africa: Thummin Printing.

Endnotes

1   Grigg, Viv. (2010). Hovering Spirit, Creative Voice, Empowered Transformation: A Retrospective. In *Living Mission*, Scott Bessnecker Ed. IVP Books. pp 23-35. (2012). Reprinted in *The New Urban World Journal*. Vol 1:1. Stephen Burris, Ed. Bangkok: International Society of Urban Mission. www.newurbanworld.org

2   http://urbanleaders.org/ma/Proposal/CommonUnderstandings/2014/program_proposal-2013edits.doc

3   Grigg, Viv. ed. (2000). *Creating an Auckland Business Theology*. Auckland: Urban Leadership Foundation.

4   Grigg, Viv. (2017). Report: *Design of Cell-Based Delivery of MATUL Content to Slum Pastors*. Report on Creative Teaching Grant, Azusa Pacific Seminary.

5   Grigg, Viv. 1986 *Servants: A Protestant Apostolic Order*. Unpublished master's paper, Fuller Theological Seminary.

6   Grigg, Viv (2000) *Worker Competency Profile*. http://www.urbanleaders.org/ma/CoreDocs/educationalconcepts.htm

7   http://www.andragogy.net/

8   Freire's pedagogy was deep-rooted and substantiated by his Christian faith, which provided him the inspiration to work relentlessly to denounce all systems of oppression that dehumanize people and steal their agency and to announce the sacredness of life which implies dignity for all. – Débora B. Agra Junker, Founder and Director of the Cátedra Paulo Freire at Garrett-Evangelical Theological Seminary

9   Considering that the Brazilian people was not yet politically constituted, the generation of intellectuals to which Anísio Teixeira and Fernando de Azevedo belonged set about creating institutions they believed were in keeping with the nation's reality. They held that the people's educational requirements would be fulfilled by expanding the supply of schools, especially primary schools, and reorganizing higher education. The population would learn how to care for their own health and be encouraged to have a less mystical, more rational mentality, while also engaging more actively in the nation's development. (Libânia Nacif Xavier, (2012) Anísio Teixeira: On universities, research and public education. *Hist. cienc. saude-Manguinhos* vol.19 no.2 Rio de Janeiro Apr./June 2012).

10   Conn (1984:54) on Kuhn's (1962/1970) idea of paradigm and Festinger's (1959) cognitive dissonance.

11   I led a number of global and regional consultations yearly, among them: Calcutta ('92), Chicago ('91), Los Angeles ('92), Seoul ('95), Hong Kong ('96), Mumbai ('93), Delhi ('93) with these coordinators . They extended these at national and city levels. Bryan Johnson lead in other cities. A New Zealand leadership

team developed a city leaders' consultation in Wanganui in 1996 (Grigg, 1997d).

12   In a letter towards the end of his life (Iremonger, 1948).

13   Brevard Childs (1970) traces it from the early 1940's to its decline in the 1960's. Because the crossover from literary analysis occurred at multiple points globally, the emergence of narrative theology occurred through multiple sources. Van Engen comments, "One realise(s) it is practically a misnomer to speak of a narrative theology "movement." The presuppositions, methodologies, agendas and styles of the players in narrative theology are too diverse to be lumped into a single cohesive movement" (1996). Yet it infuses theological thinking.

14   Both liberal and evangelical theologies are rationalist in style and foundational in approach. Where they differ is the basis of that foundationalism. Liberal theologians view the ability of the human intellect as able to discern the foundations. For evangelical theologians the foundation is the Scriptures as revealed truth (Marsden, 1997:98).

15   Brueggemann seeks to develop a post-liberal or non-foundational approach to Old Testament studies, while recognizing the collapse of trust in historical foundationalism (1997:84-87).

16   Both liberal and evangelical theologies are rationalist in style and foundational in approach. Where they differ is the basis of that foundationalism. Liberal theologians view the ability of the human intellect as able to discern the foundations. For evangelical theologians, the foundation is the Scriptures as revealed truth (Marsden, 1997:98).

17   "Just as modern epistemology was dominated by an image, that of a building needing to be supported, so postmodern epistemology is dominated by a picture: W.V.O. Quines' image of knowledge as a web or net" (Murphy, 1997:27).

18   Details from discussion with Les Allen, partner in Gaze Burt, May 2005.

19   www.urbanleaders.org/Portfolio.htm

20   Taylor, Louise. (2011). Rethinking priorities: Making time for transformational conversations [online]. *Early Education*, Vol. 50, Spring/Summer 2011: 15-18. Availability: https://search.informit.com.au/documentSummary;dn=716339874979724;res=IELNZC ISSN: 1172-9112. [cited 05 Jul 18].

21   https://www.newcommglobal.com/upload/VTHallTonna%20Values%20Map%20(1).pdf

22   For a practical primer, see Gronlund, Norman and Susan Brookhart. (2008) *Writing Instructional Objectives*. 8th Edn. Pearson.

23 https://www.learning-styles-online.com/overview/index.php

24   http://urbanleaders.org/620Leadership/01introductions/nine_paradigmsl.htm

25   Edmiston, John. *Internet Cafes for the Unreached*. https://www.cybermissions.org/icafe/Accessed Oct 15, 2018.

26   http://www.worldometers.info/world-population/india-population/ (August 8, 2018).

27   http://censusindia.gov.in/2011-Common/CensusData2011.html (August 8, 2018).

28   https://www.businesstoday.in/current/economy-politics/india-has-highest-number-of-people-living-below-poverty-line-world-bank/story/238085.html (August 10, 2018)

29   https://timesofindia.indiatimes.com/home/education/news/unemployment-rate-in-india-nearly-31-million-indians-are-jobless/articleshow/63182015.cms (August 10, 2018).

30   https://www.cbc.ca/news/world/india-census-says-1-in-6-lives-in-unsanitary-slums-1.1403897 (August 10, 2018).

31   http://pib.nic.in/newsite/PrintRelease.aspx?relid=126326 (August 8, 2018).

32   K. Rajendran, (c2015). *The Importance of Grassroots Training: Developing Grassroots Leadership*, Paper presented in an IIM Grassroots Seminar at Balasore, India pg. 3.

33   .Dr. Anuj Patro, worked with Operation Mobilization for almost 30 years among various urban and rural communities in India (May 7, 2015).

34   Herbert Hoefer. (2001) *Churchless Christianity*. Pasadena, CA: William Carey Library. pp. x-xii.

35   Patro, Anuj. May 7, 2015.

36   Dr. C. Barnabas. (2000). "Consultation on Missionary Training - Report by the Secretary" *India Journal of Missiology*, (April 2000) 13.

37   Dr. Rajendra is a contemporary Indian missiologist, who has written mission books and articles. He was the General Secretary of India Missions Association for 15 years and travelled all over India.

38   K. Rajendran, (c2017). *The Importance of Grassroots Training: Developing Grassroots Leadership*, Paper presented in an IIM Grassroots Seminar at Balasore, India (n.d.) 4.

39   Ralph D. Winter, "The New Macedonia:A Revolutionary New Era in Mission Begins," in *Perspectives on the World Christian Movements*, edited by Ralph D. Winter and Stevan C. Hawthrorne (Pasadena, CA: William Carey Library, 1981): 295.

40   K. Imotemjen Aier, *A Local Church in Action*. *ICGO*. Vol. 6, NO.2. April - June (1984) 29.

41   Data Collected from Rev. Kiran Wesley, the Associate Director for Mission India Ministry Department (August 9, 2018).

42   Rev. Susanta Patra. (2000). "*Suvartiks* (Grassroots

Level) Training. *India Journal of Missiology.* April 2000. p.17.

43   http://censusindia.gov.in/2011-prov-results/paper2/data_files/india/Rural_Urban_2011.pdf.

44   Sukhadeve, Satish. (2018). Coordinator of CBTT (August 9, 2018).

45   *If Jesus Taught Online,* quoted in APU Online training.

46   Burnsted, Brian, (2010). Online Universities Retention Rates, *USNews.* https://www.usnews.com/education/online-education/articles/2010/10/22/online-universities-retention-rate-data

47   Sears, Andrew, (2018). *GC4 and Alternative Models for Christian Accreditation for the Majority World,* slide 84. Slideshare. Accessed July 7, 2018.

48   Grigg, Viv (2000) *Worker Competency Profile.* http://www.urbanleaders.org/ma/CoreDocs/educationalconcepts.htm]

49   https://upload.wikimedia.org/wikipedia/commons/8/83/Bloom%27s_Rose.png

50   Edmiston, John. *Internet Cafes for the Unreached.* https://www.cybermissions.org/icafe/Accessed Oct 15, 2018.

51   Sears, A (2016). Personal Strategy Principles from Case Studies. *Disruptive Innovation.* Udemy slide presentation, Accessed July 7, 2018.

52   *Spirituality in post-Postmodern Metropolises* http://www.authorstream.com/Presentation/vivgrigg-1360754-kingpostmodern/

Made in the USA
Middletown, DE
03 September 2024

60326041R00075